Technology Leaders

Peter S. Cohan

- *The* fast track route to understanding and implementing the best ideas from the world's top technology businesses

- Covers all key aspects of technology leadership, from open technology to entrepreneurial leadership, and from boundaryless product development to resource allocation

- Examples, cases and ideas from the world's greatest technology companies, including Hewlett Packard, Cisco, IBM, Schlumberger, Gillette and Merck

- Includes a glossary of key concepts and a comprehensive resources guide

>> EXPRESS EXEC.COM <<

essential management thinking at your fingertips

The right of Peter S. Cohan to be identified as the author of this work has been asserted in accordance with the Copyright, Designs and Patents Act 1988

First published 2002 by
Capstone Publishing (A Wiley Company)
8 Newtec Place
Magdalen Road
Oxford OX4 1RE
United Kingdom
http://www.capstoneideas.com

CIP catalogue records for this book are available from the British Library and the US Library of Congress

ISBN 1-84112-381-1

This book is printed on acid-free paper

Substantial discounts on bulk quantities of Capstone books are available to corporations, professional associations and other organizations. Please contact Capstone for more details on +44 (0)1865 798 623 or (fax) +44 (0)1865 240 941 or (e-mail) info@wiley-capstone.co.uk

Contents

Introduction to ExpressExec

ExpressExec is 3 million words of the latest management thinking compiled into 10 modules. Each module contains 10 individual titles forming a comprehensive resource of current business practice written by leading practitioners in their field. From brand management to balanced scorecard, ExpressExec enables you to grasp the key concepts behind each subject and implement the theory immediately. Each of the 100 titles is available in print and electronic formats.

Through the ExpressExec.com Website you will discover that you can access the complete resource in a number of ways:

» printed books or e-books;
» e-content – PDF or XML (for licensed syndication) adding value to an intranet or Internet site;
» a corporate e-learning/knowledge management solution providing a cost-effective platform for developing skills and sharing knowledge within an organization;
» bespoke delivery – tailored solutions to solve your need.

Why not visit www.expressexec.com and register for free key management briefings, a monthly newsletter and interactive skills checklists. Share your ideas about ExpressExec and your thoughts about business today.

Please contact elound@wiley-capstone.co.uk for more information.

Introduction to Technology Leaders

Who are the technology leaders and why are they important? This chapter considers the notable characteristics of technology leaders, including:

» what distinguishes a technology leader from its peers; and
» what distinguishes the performance of the technology leaders.

In the Darwinian struggle for profitable growth, there is something to be learned from America's most highly evolved companies. Companies that come out on top of the fastest growing, most rapidly changing, and most intellectually demanding markets have something to teach the rest of the business world.

America's most highly evolved companies are *technology leaders*. Technology permeates industry. It is the basis for many commercial and consumer products, and is a key enabler for service provision. However, great technology alone is not enough to create a successful business. Uncounted billions have been spent developing technology that ultimately did not generate positive cash flows. On the other hand, a select group of technology entrepreneurs has become wealthy, converting tiny investments into vast personal fortunes. Part of this dynamic is a natural outgrowth of capitalism's cycle of creative destruction.

As they develop, many companies go through fairly predictable phases. Initially, company founders rely on at most three sources of cash: personal money, paying customers, and possibly investment capital. To maintain positive cash flow they focus on external factors such as changing customer needs, advances in technology, competitor strategies, and investor requirements. As these companies grow, they borrow money from banks, issue stock, create divisions, acquire some businesses and divest others. An unintended side-effect of their success is a distraction from the very behavior that created it in the first place - the focus on maintaining positive cash flow by adapting to the needs of the marketplace.

In many cases, key decision makers delegate the responsibility for adapting the company to changing customer needs, advances in technology, and evolving competitor strategies. These executives spend increasing amounts of time mediating disputes over transfer pricing, arguing over executive compensation, trading businesses, redrawing organization charts and catering to the needs of powerful board members

As a result, they create an opportunity for a new generation of entrepreneurs to take away their customers. By the time the large company executives notice that anything has changed, they are years behind the "value propositions" offered by the new generation of entrepreneurs. Although these large companies are able to survive, often for many years, they have lost the strategic initiative in their industries and, as a result, can only rely on cost reduction, not revenue growth, to enhance profitability.

Some large companies, however, are able to transcend this cycle. Consider the trajectories of IBM and Hewlett-Packard during the 1980s and 1990s. Over the last 20 years, dramatic changes occurred in their markets, including the growing importance of the personal computer, the change from proprietary mainframe-based corporate computer systems to open client/server architectures, and the increased role of applications software.

IBM was unable to respond to these changes effectively. It remained dependent on the less robust proprietary mainframe business, ceded the personal computer operating system and application market to Microsoft, and focused management attention on internal reorganizations. Its senior executives were replaced and its stock price, having peaked at 180 in 1987, dropped as low as 40 in 1993. Although IBM's financial position has recovered significantly under its new CEO, it remains to be seen whether the company will be able to retake the strategic initiative that it formerly enjoyed.

In contrast, HP combined its discovery of inkjet technology with an aggressive marketing strategy to build a 60% share of the $10bn worldwide market for laser printers. HP also built a fast growing line of UNIX-based computers to act as servers for networks of personal computers and workstations. Furthermore, its share of the personal computer market is continuing to rise. As a result, 90% of HP's revenues are derived from products introduced within the last four years. Between 1991 and 1995, HP's stock price increased 480%.

What does HP do that IBM did not? This work explores how 20 technology companies, like HP, have sustained their success. The 20 companies were selected from a sample of 1309 US companies based on their high R&D as a percentage of sales, their leading five-year average return on equity relative to their industry, and their reputation for innovative products and services.

They have a truly impressive track record. For example, between 1990 and 1995, they earned return on equity that was *2.4 times* the US industry median. They increased shareholder value at a rate *4.5 times* that of the Barra Index of all US securities. And they generated profits per employee that were *4.1 times* the US industry median. What is perhaps most impressive is that they were able to achieve all this profitability while growing revenues at *5.7 times* the US industry median. Furthermore, during this five year period, these outstanding companies *grew earnings per share at a 43% compound annual growth rate*, while the US industry median actually dropped at an 11% rate.

The companies are Amgen, Cisco Systems, Compaq Computer, EMC Corporation, Gillette, Heartstream (which was acquired by Hewlett-Packard in 1997), Hewlett-Packard, Intel, International Flavors & Fragrances, Johnson & Johnson, Merck, Micron Technology, Microsoft, Minnesota Mining, Oracle, Parametric Technology, Schlumberger, Synopsys, Thermo Electron, and US Robotics (which was acquired by 3Com and whose Palm unit was successfully spun off from 3Com in 2000).

In the last five years, some of these companies have surged ahead, others have made steady progress, and a few have fallen from their leadership perch. For example, Cisco Systems grew so fast between 1995 and 2000 that in March 2000, its $500bn stock market capitalization made it the most valuable company in the world. In the year that followed, Cisco Systems tumbled along with the collapse of the dot-coms and upstart telecommunications companies – wiping out $350bn in market capitalization. By contrast, Microsoft saw its value grow steadily, suffering some decline as a result of a major antitrust trial which threatened to break up Microsoft. By 2001, with the change in political administration, fears of the break up evaporated and Microsoft's market position surged, as it sat ready to consolidate its market position with its $25bn cash hoard.

All 20 of these companies may not remain technology leaders in the future; however, the management principles that they followed to become technology leaders will endure and the companies that adhere to these principles are likely to prevail.

Definition of Terms

Technology leaders have introduced new management processes, the understanding of which demands an understanding of new management concepts. This chapter defines elements of the new management vocabulary including:

» success cycles; and
» the four sources of advantage that drive superior return on innovation.

The most important factor that keeps these 20 companies ahead of the pack is the way they adapt to change. Rather than deny that change is taking place, technology leaders look for ways to exploit change for the benefit of their customers. If this change means that some products must become obsolete, they cannibalize ruthlessly. And technology leaders don't just cannibalize their products, they even uproot their most fundamental business processes.

Technology leaders work with a mental model that guides their strategic choices. In this model (see Fig. 2.1), people and technology are combined to create products that customers are eager to buy. These products generate capital and insight. The capital comes from the products' operating profit. The insight is the result of feedback from customers, competitors, and the effectiveness of the firm's execution. Through resource allocation, technology leaders channel this capital and insight into new product development projects and business process redesign.

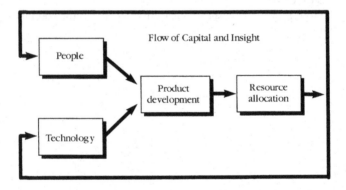

Fig. 2.1 Technology leaders' success cycles.

By optimizing this model, technology leaders create a success cycle that leads to ever greater levels of capital and insight. Technology leaders expand this success cycle by drawing on four sources of

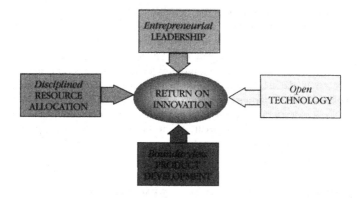

Fig. 2.2 Four sources of advantage.

advantage (see Fig. 2.2) that drive ever higher levels of return on innovation.

ENTREPRENEURIAL LEADERSHIP

Technology leaders identify, attract and motivate the smartest people to perform to the limits of their ability. How do they do this? They have CEOs who combine a deep understanding of technology with an intense drive to make money. They use values-based visions that grab smart people and pull them in the right direction. This contrasts with peer companies who try to motivate people by exhorting them to "maximize shareholder value." Technology leaders have open organizations and they take a humanistic approach to managing people. However, technology leaders have some hard edges. They are highly competitive and they pay people to perform. They often balance below-average cash compensation with stock options that are valuable only if the company's stock price keeps going up.

OPEN TECHNOLOGIES

Technology leaders get the technology that meets the needs of their customers. In this pursuit, they often pay up for quick access. If they have the technology inside the company, they will invest to make it even more valuable to customers. If the technology is available from outside the firm, they will get access to it. This access could range from acquiring a company to licensing the technology from the people who developed it. Technology leaders seek a strong market position in specific "leverage point technologies" that will allow them to organize third parties in pursuit of an industry standard. In addition, technology leaders assign people to monitor new technologies before they become a dangerous threat. At the same time, they catalog their non-core technologies and outplace them, while selectively "renting" technologies that are needed only for specific projects.

BOUNDARYLESS PRODUCT DEVELOPMENT

Technology leaders combine their people and technology in a process that generates superior value for customers. They form cross-functional teams. They work with early-adopters to understand their unmet needs. They develop prototypes based on these needs. And they modify these prototypes based on customer feedback. Furthermore, they create "product supply" capabilities that enable them to meet mass market demand while maintaining high product quality and delivery time standards.

DISCIPLINED RESOURCE ALLOCATION

Technology leaders use the capital and insight that results from their successful products to expand their success cycles. They use resource allocation to spread organizational learning. They screen projects using portfolio grids. They build project timelines for the most attractive projects that incorporate specific exit ramps. They estimate success probabilities and incremental net cash flows between decision nodes. And they systematically reallocate resources to the projects with the greatest expected value.

RETURN ON INNOVATION

This is the present value of the cash flow components of a research project, including:

» cost of feasibility research;
» cost of licensing in technologies for the project, if any;
» cost of prototype development, including usability and manufacturability testing;
» cost of regulatory testing, if applicable;
» cost of incremental production facilities, if any;
» cost of incremental product distribution network, if any; and
» contribution margin of new product resulting from the research project over its life.

In order to calculate return on innovation for an entire company, the return on innovation for all its projects is added together as well as the costs associated with research projects that do not result in marketable products.

The four strategic choices all work together to increase the value of the firm. They reduce wasted spending. They shorten product cycle times, thus accelerating the cash inflows from new products. They even increase the magnitude of the cash flows from new products.

Entrepreneurial leadership ensures a steady stream of new products – and the positive cash flows that they generate – while managing the growth in the cash outflows associated with the research staff.

» **Decreases cash outflows.** Technology leaders have fewer people, being paid lower base salaries, who do more work. As a result, they have lower employee cash costs than their peers.
» **Shortens time to generate cash inflows.** Technology leaders can get products to market in less time. Highly motivated, smart people are able to focus their energies intensely on achieving ambitious project deadlines without sacrificing product quality.

Open technology broadens the markets into which technologies are sold. As a result, *open* technology brings more cash into the company. Technology leaders shed or outplace non-core technologies – thereby turning off the cash spigot to lower return technologies. And they outsource alliance technologies. This process helps increase the cash inflows from new products by getting better products to market faster. It also limits the firm's costs for technologies that the company needs for a short time.

» **Decreases cash outflows.** Technology leaders stop spending on technologies that have outlived their ability to create value for customers. Technology leaders channel the cash thus saved to technologies with greater potential to create value.

» **Shortens time to generate cash inflows.** Technology leaders reduce product cycle times. Rather than delay a project to develop a key technology internally, they license it from a third party. As a result, technology leaders get products to market faster and begin generating positive cash flow sooner.

» **Increases magnitude of cash inflows.** Technology leaders get incremental sources of cash by finding new markets for core technologies, and/or by licensing out non-core technologies in exchange for royalties or other fees.

Boundaryless product development increases return on innovation by decreasing cash outflows, shortening time to market, and increasing operating profit.

» **Decreases cash outflows.** Technology leaders don't incur the extensive rework associated with the "relay race" approach to product development. As a result, the costs associated with redesign to ease manufacturing and to increase market acceptance are eliminated. As a result, *boundaryless* product development process decreases cash outflows.

» **Shortens time to generate cash inflows.** Technology leaders shorten the time from the start of the project to product launch. Again, by eliminating rework associated with "missed" hand-offs in the relay race approach, time to market is shortened. This speeds up the time to generate positive cash flow and, because the cash is received earlier, increases its value to the company.

» **Increases magnitude of cash inflows.** Technology leaders produce and market products that are more successful in the market place. As a result, they get more operating profit.

Disciplined resource allocation increases the magnitude of the positive net cash flows that the research portfolio will generate. It also shifts resources out of projects with unacceptable prospects for success – thus minimizing cash outflows.

» **Decreases cash outflows.** Technology leaders cancel projects with limited potential before too much money has been spent. As a result, investment in innovation is targeted at projects with the highest potential returns.

» **Shortens time to generate cash inflows.** By ensuring that the most promising projects are not deprived of resources, technology leaders complete projects more quickly. As a result, products get to market faster and begin generating operating profits sooner.

» **Increases magnitude of cash inflows.** By supplying the most promising projects with the capital and other resources they need, technology leaders create more successful products. As a result, operating profit increases.

The Evolution of Technological Innovation

Technological innovation has driven human progress since the discovery of fire. This chapter examines technological innovation over the last 100 years. It includes:

» a brief essay on the driving forces of technological innovation over the last 100 years; and
» a timeline that traces key technological innovations – and related management breakthroughs – from 1900 to 1999.

The evolution of technology in society over the last century is really a story of brilliant individuals who created breakthroughs that enhanced the quality of life. The notion of innovation as something that can be managed is of more recent vintage.

Consider the state of technological innovation 101 years ago. In 1900, Henry Adams visited the Great Exposition in Paris. A new bridge, the Alexandre III, spanned the River Seine near exhibition halls, the Grand Palais and the Petit Palais, that displayed contemporary artwork. The Paris Metro had just opened, with its Art Nouveau ironwork entrances. The Eiffel Tower, completed a decade earlier, punctuated the skyline.

Adams returned to the exhibit halls repeatedly to visit the Gallery of Machines and its 40-foot-tall dynamo. There, he wrote in *The Education of Henry Adams*, "the planet itself seemed less impressive, in its old-fashioned, deliberate, annual, or daily revolution, than this huge wheel, revolving within arm's length at some vertiginous speed." On considering the achievements of science and technology, Adams found his "historical neck broken by the sudden irruption of forces totally new."

Many historical necks have broken since then. The recently completed century had inventions and innovations, many of which have had a huge impact. In some instances, that impact has been obvious – the explosion of the A-bombs over Hiroshima and Nagasaki. In others, it is more subtle – the ones and zeros that keep computers and telecommunications working.

In the twentieth century, a change in how work is organized, the development of new materials, and the adoption of information technology have altered what workers produce and how they work. Advances in transport and communications have kept people moving and have fulfilled the desire to cross new frontiers, even in space. New sources of energy, from gasoline to nuclear fission, provided the power. New products and industries allowed consumers to fill their homes and occupy their leisure time. And the creation of drugs, diagnostic tools, and medical procedures reduced mortality and enhanced the quality of life.

Innovation can be a process in which the benefits emerge slowly. Thomas Edison electrified Pearl Street in lower Manhattan in 1882, and it was 30 years before electric appliances were marketed to homemakers. Nevertheless, the pace of innovation picked up in the twentieth century – and continues to do so. While the US does not have a monopoly on inventiveness, it has been the main locus of innovation since the 1930s.

Both Western Europe and Japan focused on post-World War II rebuilding; later, economic rigidities in Europe constrained innovation, while the pace of innovation accelerated in Japan as new technologies and new methods of production were refined. In the US, six factors have prevailed since the 1930s: ample natural resources, a mass market, a large workforce, an influx of scientists from Europe and the rest of the world, an interplay between private-sector and university research, and federal dollars funding university work.

Innovation in the twentieth century was driven by two goals. The first was the desire to achieve speed. The second was a focus on scale – whether the most efficient size of company, the largest market for a product, or the smallest storage space for information.

Cutting travel time demonstrates the will to achieve speed. The Wright brothers flew their biplane at 6.8mph over Kill Devil Hills, NC in 1903. Forty-four years later, Chuck Yeager broke the sound barrier, flying the X-1 test plane high above the Mojave Desert at 670mph. The push for speed is found everywhere: making things faster, selling faster, buying faster, and processing information faster.

Henry Ford embodied the view that time is money. By speeding up production to lower costs, his assembly line permitted Ford to cut car prices and raise wages. As a result, scale changed society: the German automobile manufacturers were selling cars in the 1890s, well before Ford, but for many years they viewed their potential market as small and elite.

The interaction of speed and scale has motivated innovation in many cases. New products undergo constant improvements, becoming cheaper and more available. That spurs demand, more refinements, and, usually, further price cuts. The mass market was one of the most critical developments of the twentieth century, one that allowed others to emerge.

There were certainly important innovations prior to the twentieth century. For example, eyeglasses in fifteenth century Italy enabled individuals to overcome myopia or presbyopia and become more productive. In the late nineteenth century, electric light lengthened the day's usable hours, enhancing both work and leisure.

It is clear that the gains from innovation in this century have grown significantly. Speed and scale had much to do with that. So, too, did the drive to understand and tame Nature, to view progress through science as the "endless frontier" that President Franklin D. Roosevelt's science advisor, Vannevar Bush, wrote about in 1945. Why sharpen vision with artificial lenses when it's possible to reshape the cornea with lasers or even replace it entirely? Why build radios and computers with bulky, power-hungry vacuum tubes, when thousands of solid-state tubes, or transistors, can be etched on the head of a microchip?

In 1965, Gordon E. Moore, a co-founder of Intel, predicted that microchip power would double every 18 months, with a corresponding 50% decline in costs. But the success of Moore's Law has not has not precluded technological mistakes. The Hindenburg exploded, the Spruce Goose lumbered, Sony fumbled Betamax. The century has also created technological horrors, often for military reasons. Chemical warfare killed French troops during the Great War, V-2 rockets struck Londoners during the Blitz, two atomic bombs were dropped on the Japanese, and napalm devastated villagers in Vietnam.

The knowledge at the root of science and technology is value-free. However, Lewis Mumford, the American social critic, believed that people both shape and are shaped by technological change. While the globe may be one mass market, the World Wide Web and e-commerce have shown that it is divisible into many market segments. People value speed, so new chips and glass fibers are accelerating the transfer of information. And the scale of exploration varies dramatically – from space to the sequences of the genetic code. In 100 years, science and technology have advanced further than Henry Adams could ever have imagined.

Here are some key milestones in the twentieth century evolution of technological innovation and management

> **1900 Research laboratory.** General Electric creates America's first major industrial lab in a carriage house in Schenectady,

N.Y. General Electric's chief engineer, German immigrant Charles P. Steinmetz, spurred the creation of America's first major industrial research lab. Begun in December, 1900, in a carriage house behind Steinmetz's rooming house in Schenectady, N.Y., it soon moved to bigger quarters. Within 15 years, the staff of researchers had swelled to 300 and was churning out innovations in X-ray equipment, radio, lighting, and more. Officials from DuPont, General Motors, and Eastman Kodak sought out lab director Willis Whitney for advice on how to organize research. In the 1930s, the lab's work was featured in radio broadcasts and traveling shows, and it became known as the House of Magic.

- **1901 US Steel formed**, with $1bn in capital, through a merger of 10 companies.
- **1907 Bakelite.** Chemist Leo Baekeland creates the first synthetic manmade substance.
- **1907 Triode.** Inventor Lee De Forest patents the triode, one of the earliest vacuum tubes.
- **1910 Synthetic rubber.** Bayer begins small-scale production of synthesized rubber in Germany.
- **1911 Taylorism.** Frederick Winslow Taylor publishes *Principles of Scientific Management*. Philadelphia-born Frederick Winslow Taylor, the son of a lawyer, became a machinist whose factory-floor observations prompted him to criticize workers who "soldiered" – the slackers of his day. *Principles of Scientific Management* offered solutions for improving industrial efficiency, from piecework incentives to time cards and worksheets. In the US, managers paid attention, while workers were suspicious. In Soviet Russia, leaders eager to industrialize a mostly agrarian society in the 1920s and 1930s embraced Taylor's notion that "the system must be first." American engineers influenced by both Taylor and Henry Ford advised on the construction of giant complexes such as Magnitogorsk, the steelmaking center in the Ural Mountains.
- **1913 Assembly line.** Henry Ford introduces the first moving assembly line at his Model T plant in Highland Park, MI. In the

late nineteenth century, Chicago meatpackers used overhead trolleys to move carcasses along as they cut them, while food canners used conveyor belts to process food. But Henry Ford took the concept to a higher level. When he introduced the first moving assembly line in 1913 at his Model T plant in Highland Park, MI, Ford's goal was efficiency, speed, and a mass market. Different conveyor systems smoothly carried components to the main assembly line. Before the assembly line, a Model T took 12 hours to produce and cost $950. By 1927, Model Ts were being produced in half that time, at a unit price of $290.

» **1925 Bell Labs** is opened at 625 West Street in New York.

» **1934 Nylon.** DuPont chemist Wallace C. Carothers develops nylon.

» **1942 Xerox.** Physicist Chester Carlson receives a patent for the process of electrophotography that led to the Xerox machine.

» **1945 Science: The Endless Frontier.** In his report, Vannevar Bush advocates strong government support of university research.

» **1946 ENIAC.** The giant ENIAC computer is officially dedicated.

» **1947 Transistor.** Walter Brattain, John Bardeen, and William Shockley discover the transistor. It looks like a few metal scraps and a paper clip, but it initiated the silicon revolution that shaped industry in the second half of the twentieth century. *The New York Times* showed little excitement when it reported in June, 1948, that "a device called a transistor, which has several applications in radio where a vacuum tube ordinarily is employed, was demonstrated for the first time yesterday . . . " The device gave off little heat and offered power savings over vacuum tubes. When the first mass-produced transistor radios appeared in 1954, they failed, because of their then-expensive $49.95 price. However, within a decade, the transistor was used in products such as computers and guided missiles. Bell Laboratories inventors Walter Brattain, John Bardeen, and William Shockley shared the 1956 Nobel prize for physics for their discovery.

» **1953 IBM introduces the first of 700 series of computers.**

» **1956 Sociologist William Whyte publishes *The Organiza-tion Man*.**

» **1959 Robot manufacturing.** A robotic arm is first used in industry, at a General Electric plant.

» **1961 IBM begins selling its "golf ball" Selectric typewriter.**

» **1967 Microchip.** An early IBM chip hints at the coming semiconductor revolution. The semiconductor industry was started by the invention of the transistor. Integrated circuits were constructed with millions of transistors. Silicon circuits exhibited new potential in 1971 with Intel's development of the first microprocessor. That chip had 2300 transistors. Microprocessors made possible the personal computer. And transistor counts mushroomed: Intel's core Pentium III chip, introduced in 2000, has 9.5 million transistors.

» **1970s Supercomputer.** Cray Research launches supercomputers for extraordinarily complex tasks.

» **1971 First microprocessor made by Intel.**

» **1982 Japanese auto manufacturer Honda begins auto production at Marysville, OH.**

» **1986 Microsoft goes public.**

» **1993 Michael Hammer and James Champy publish *Re-engineering the Corporation*.**

» **1993 Marc Andreessen and team develop the Mosaic internet browser, forerunner of Netscape Navigator, at the University of Illinois at Urbana-Champaign.**

» **1997 Thinking Machines?** Chess champion Garry Kasparov loses his rematch with IBM's Deep Blue computer.

» **1998 US business investment in information technology accounts for 34% of total equipment spending and grew at an inflation-adjusted annual rate of 25% between 1998 and 2000, only to decline in 2001.**

» **1999 Internet.** The Internet is transformed from a resource for government and university researchers to a worldwide medium used by about 160 million people. In 1990 it was a resource for government agencies and university researchers. In 2000, an estimated 160 million people around the world are logging on to the Internet, and the number could reach 500 million by 2003. Meanwhile, consumers and businesses spent $50bn online in 1998. The Internet has changed life and work – from how people buy plane tickets and what people read, to how the workplace functions. A key driving force was the advent in 1991 of the World Wide Web, which combined the electronic, the communications, and the visual ages into one.

The idea of the Internet took hold in the 1960s, when computer expert J.C.R. Licklider of the Defense Department's Advanced Research Projects Agency talked about "an experimental network of multi-access computers" that would create "communities" of common interest. If it worked out, said Licklider, "surely the boon to humankind would be beyond measure."

While this timeline suggests the important role of brilliant inventors in the evolution of technology, the notion that technological innovation can be managed is a relatively recent phenomenon. As we discuss here, a relatively small number of companies such as Hewlett-Packard, 3M, and others have created cultures that encourage innovation – thereby transcending the abilities of any individual inventor. One of the key issues we address here is that there are often limits to how well a large organization can sustain its leadership as new technologies emerge that threaten their market position.

As the timeline illustrates, in many cases the inventor who develops a new technology is able to capture its value. In other cases, a larger company is able to usurp that value from the original inventor.

The E-Dimension

Technology leaders eat their own cooking. This chapter shows how technology leaders use e-commerce to best advantage. It includes:

» Cisco's Cisco Connection Online case;
» IBM's e-engineering of its HR activities; and
» five best practices of e-business.

An important characteristic shared by technology leaders is their ability to use new technologies in their own operations to enhance their competitiveness. One of the best examples of such adoption comes from Cisco Systems' use of the Internet. Specifically, Cisco Systems' Cisco Connection Online (CCO) is among the most profitable applications of e-business. In examining the CCO case, we will explore the reason CCO was created, how it works, what results it has produced, and where it may be going in the future. From this discussion emerge some important best practices for the adoption of the e-dimension as implemented by technology leaders.

Cisco Systems' 2000 revenues totaled $24bn. Eighty percent of these sales were generated over CCO. Cisco Systems estimated that in 1999, CCO added $1.5bn to Cisco's profits.

CCO HISTORY

Cisco began the development of the Web site in 1993, when it also formed a team of three to four people to identify ways to enhance productivity in technical support. Cisco had heard of a browser tool called Mosaic, from the University of Illinois. In 1994, Cisco began to use the Mosaic browser and an Apache Web server. At the time, companies tended not to do b-to-b commerce over the Net. The Net was considered to be for government use only. Cisco called the Web site cio.cisco.com (cio stood for Customer Information Online).

Cisco used cio.cisco.com to put its technical information on the Web. Using the same system, customers asked questions, which were analyzed by the system and then linked to a likely response. The system also allowed customers to download software. Within 18 months, 70% of technical support questions could be handled by the system. Using this system, Cisco Systems was rated the best in the industry in customer satisfaction, while tightly managing the cost of its support operation.

In 1995, Cisco connected its partners, customers, and resellers to the system, thus creating the networked model of conducting business. This business model change led cio.cisco.com to evolve into CCO. Cisco also decided to expand b-to-b e-commerce to include giving customers information on the status of their order. In August 1995, Cisco introduced the first version of this "window into the company" and evaluated its effectiveness, revising the system every three months. Subsequently Cisco introduced several e-commerce tools that the company revised every six months based on feedback from users. This system became the largest e-commerce application in the world. In 1996 CCO's annual revenues were $1bn, in 1997 $2bn, and in 1998 $5.7bn.

The success of CCO was based on three initiatives: (1) Cisco developed the technology needed to fulfill the requirements of the application; (2) Cisco created an equal partnership between the information technology (IT) department and the business; and (3) Cisco focused on customer wants. In fact, Cisco's IT department created a subunit called E-Commerce Ambassador, whose job it is to go out to resellers and large direct customers and find out how Cisco can do a better job of doing business electronically.

Cisco's IT department has been able to do more than others for several reasons. First, many other IT departments are caught up with operating or replacing legacy back-end systems, working on the Year 2000 problem, or installing SAP. These initiatives consume so much time that IT departments do not have time to look for breakthroughs. Because Cisco did not have legacy systems, it could build CCO unimpeded from scratch.

Second, CCO was not an IT initiative. In most companies, there is a big gap between IT, business functions, and executive management. At Cisco, there is a high degree of alignment toward building tools to solve customer problems. Cisco's IT department talks to European resellers, British Telecom, and other large customers. Because Cisco is aligned in this way, it has fast cycle times. Cisco's IT department can release a version of the system in 60 days, try it for 30 days, and refine it based on that feedback. Cisco is a fast-turnaround, fast-feedback corporation.

According to *Internet Computing*, in September 1998 CCO allowed Cisco's 45,000 customers around the world to gain real-time information on price, availability, configuration requirements, ordering, invoice status and validation, and shipments of complex internetworking products.

Cisco customers can forward procurement information to their own employees for modification and approval via CCO's e-mail features. Customers can also access product specifications, join discussion forums, receive bug alerts, and download software patches and tools.

Cisco estimates that it now takes 15 to 60 minutes for a buyer to enter a clean order through CCO and for Cisco to complete the process by directing it into its back-end system for production. This compares favorably with a process that took days or weeks in the past when Cisco's own sales force and support staff and the purchasing managers of its customers were tied up in paperwork to process an invoice that was often full of errors.

According to Susan Aragon-Stemel, manager of networked commerce information systems at Cisco, rather than sending Cisco customers CDs or documentation, CCO implemented a download feature for software kits and tools that as of February 1998 was estimated to have saved Cisco $80mn a year.

Whereas the benefits of CCO to Cisco are clear, the reaction from customers is not overly enthusiastic. Some Cisco customers view placing and checking orders electronically as a natural progression, regardless of any prodding from Cisco. Digex, an ISP based in Beltsville, Maryland, has ordered millions of dollars' worth of Cisco equipment each quarter. Christopher McCleary, the former CEO of Digex, felt that Cisco was pushing its customers and getting them to adopt online ordering primarily to lower Cisco's costs.

Despite being generally supportive of CCO and Cisco's e-commerce strategy, some customers are hard-pressed to determine the exact benefits of ordering products from the vendor via the Internet versus faxing in a purchase order or using electronic data interchange (EDI).

Another Cisco customer, Boeing, points out that although Cisco is reducing its overhead by streamlining its order fulfillment process, it is likely that CCO would help improve Cisco's profitability more than Boeing's. Although Boeing placed an order for $124mn worth of routers and switches for its worldwide corporate network in 1998, the company could not assess how much using CCO would reduce Boeing's overhead.

Cisco distributors, such as NCR, appreciate CCO because it gives salespeople more current information. Efficiency has improved because CCO streamlines the process of getting information from account managers to NCR. NCR perceives that CCO has helped free up Cisco account managers to spend more time closing deals. In NCR's view, its regular business relationship with Cisco continues to depend not on the details in CCO but on the network of interpersonal relationships between the two companies.

In 1998, Cisco began to roll out an offer to its top customers, such as Alcatel, NCR, and NEC. This offer consisted of a set of messaging tools that allow Cisco's customers to connect their sales force automation and purchasing systems through CCO into Cisco's database and enterprise resource planning (ERP) systems. Customers submit the valid orders to Cisco with the right configuration and pricing information. Then the resellers immediately go back to their customers and validate the orders. Cisco's objective is to place an order with a valid configuration from the start and get that order scheduled and built.

Clearly CCO is an important example of b-to-b e-commerce. And Cisco shows an important difference between the b-to-c and b-to-b segments. There are many examples of "pure play" b-to-c applications that create important rivalry dynamics between incumbents and new entrants. In the b-to-b segment, such dynamics are virtually absent. Why?

The barriers to entry for an incumbent in b-to-b e-commerce are virtually insurmountable. It would be difficult, if not impossible, to convince a business executive to allow an independent e-commerce firm to get in between the company and its customers. When it comes to such fundamental activities as placing orders, fulfilling orders, and providing service to customers, most business executives will continue to choose to do most of these activities, with the exception of customer service, themselves.

Of course there are compelling reasons why systems like CCO are so rare. The Web can represent a parallel channel for reaching customers. As such, in most companies, it may threaten the managers of the other parallel channels. The manager of a direct sales force, an indirect sales force, or a telephone sales force will feel uncomfortable when a new channel gets introduced.

Because the Web is most effective when it encourages functions to work together, a b-to-b e-commerce initiative creates unique management challenges. Not all companies are managed with the same philosophy that Cisco follows. At Cisco, a large percentage of employee compensation is tied to improvements in corporate scores received on independent assessments of customer satisfaction. This compensation arrangement reflects a corporate emphasis on teamwork and industry leadership that few companies can match. Therefore, whereas it might be natural for Cisco's IT and customer service departments to work together to benefit the customer, this sense of teamwork may be difficult for other companies to achieve, thus inhibiting these firms' ability to obtain the most benefit from b-to-b e-commerce.

IBM

Another great example of the use of the Internet by technology leaders is IBM's e-engineering of its employee payments. IBM followed the lead of Cisco Systems and cobbled its own shoes to help show potential customers the economic benefits of e-commerce. IBM began to realize in the mid-1990s that there was tremendous potential to use the Internet as a means of streamlining its accounts payable process. By January 1999, IBM had achieved some dramatic improvements in human resources (HR) payments and vendor processing productivity.

How were these performance improvements achieved? For the HR payments e-engineering project, IBM adopted the following practices:

» standardized payroll cycles and calendars – weekly for hourly employees and half-monthly for salaried employees;
» employed a single common employee information database for both HR and payroll;
» direct-deposited paychecks for 94% of employees;
» used automated time-collection tools and sophisticated algorithms to verify time;
» developed, communicated, and enforced a uniform T&E policy;
» processed all T&E expense reporting through a single system;
» replaced cash advances with a corporate-sponsored credit-card program; and
» used T&E expense data to negotiate discounts with vendors.

The vendor payments e-engineering process achieved its results by adopting the following best practices:

» used a procurement card;
» moved approvals and data validations up front;
» developed online catalogs and online requisitioning;

» treated purchasing and accounts payable as one process;
» extended integrated information systems to suppliers;
» involved suppliers in new-product development and value chain analysis;
» integrated purchasing, payables, and receiving computer applications; and
» used electronic commerce and electronic data interchange.

Since the details of these applications are useful for financial executives, we will explore IBM's practices in greater depth and conclude this section with an assessment of the implications of IBM's strategy here for e-commerce project financial evaluation in general. According to Robert Hughes, IBM national accounts payable services manager, the accounts payable e-engineering project was prompted by his department's receipt of a million invoices per year from its smaller suppliers. Hughes realized that IBM should practice what it preached – use e-commerce to let its smaller suppliers send IBM their invoices electronically.

In 1998, IBM formed a team made up of Global Services (IBM's business service organization), procurement, and accounts payable to develop a customized electronic invoice. IBM used Forms Exchange, a component of the Global Services network, to accomplish this objective. Now, IBM's smaller suppliers (95% of its vendors) use a standard Internet connection and a Web browser to access IBM's Web site, fill out the forms, and submit them electronically.

IBM converted the Web-based forms into EDI documents and routed them through its EDI system to accounts payable, where they are treated as if they were standard EDI transactions from IBM's larger vendors.

IBM's accounts payable department also required its employees to use paper purchase orders to buy products and services ranging from internal catering services to software. IBM had 12 separate systems for dealing with vendors, and no connection between procurement and accounts payable.

If an IBM employee wanted to buy an office chair, that person would make the request of the procurement department. Procurement then went to IBM's suppliers, picked a chair, issued a paper purchase order, and the chair was shipped. The paper invoice from the supplier later went to accounts payable. Often, the invoice did not match the purchase order, was coded inaccurately, or arrived late. So only 66% of invoices were paid when first received. The others required more information. Frustrated employees often skipped the procurement process altogether to get supplies.

Changing the process first required procurement and accounts payable to do something not done in the past – communicate. In early 1997, IBM formed a team of the appropriate people from accounts payable and purchasing. IBM brought in some suppliers and employees to join the team. The team asked the suppliers and employees for ideas on what the team could do to make it easier and more cost-effective for them to accomplish the objectives of the procurement process.

Ultimately, the 12 general procurement and accounts-payable systems were integrated into one system. The paper requisition process was replaced by an online system, which helped reduce errors and speed up the process. IBM also speeded up its process by eliminating levels of corporate approval and by increasing expense authorization limits. IBM also established a data warehouse of purchase order and payment data.

These process improvements helped procurement save $1bn for IBM. Now, 91% of invoices are paid when first received, and cost-per-invoice has dropped from $1.50 to $1.02. IBM's assistant controller Joseph Martin notes that IBM now has a very efficient system with common processes.

Another benefit of the change is that IBM uses its purchasing volumes to negotiate lower unit costs for procured items. This was achieved by the team's decision to replace paper purchase orders for high-volume orders under $200, with employee purchase cards. Employees use the cards to make purchases without authorization with an online catalog.

Automated buying currently represents 80% of IBM's procurement transactions. For the remaining 20% of IBM's higher-priced orders, a contract form with pre-approved authorization and standard terms and conditions has been developed. This new procedure cuts the time needed to place contracts from nine months to one.

IBM expects electronic procurement to reduce the cost to process an order by 80% . Hughes estimated that $1 saved in procurement was equivalent to $7 in revenue in terms of its impact on profit. Hughes believes that his group has helped create a seamless requisition-to-payment process, making it easy and flexible for the employee to procure goods and services, and for the vendor to send IBM electronic invoices and receive payment.

IBM also took a team-based approach to its employee disbursements system. Tony Angelo, IBM project executive for worldwide employee disbursements, worked with IBM's HR department in 1996 to improve employee disbursements. Prior to 1996, IBM's HR department would develop a new compensation policy, and Angelo's department would need to figure out how to administer it.

However, since IBM's HR department determines employee benefits, salary increases, and frequency of increases, Angelo wanted to work more closely with HR.

Angelo also wanted a more streamlined approach. In the 1980s in the United States, Angelo had eight payroll systems and locations in the US alone. Depending on their location, some employees were paid weekly, some biweekly. Now IBM has one system. All IBM's regular employees are paid on a half-monthly basis, and temporary employees on a weekly basis. IBM saves money by minimizing the number of times it runs the payroll over the course of the year. The new system helped cut payroll costs by 95% and reduced per-pay-distribution costs from $5.75 to $1.77.

IBM also used technology to cut T&E expenses. In the early 1990s, IBM had 25 US locations processing T&E expense reimbursements. In 1993, it consolidated them into one centralized system. As a result, processing T&E costs dropped by 83% , and the process cost per T&E expense report fell from $23.00 to $2.02.

The IBM example demonstrates the way that financial managers should be thinking about how to conduct the financial analysis of e-commerce. Financial executives should take note of several aspects of IBM's approach. IBM combined measures of process improvement with financial measures. By combining these two categories of measures, IBM was able to understand how best to achieve financial benefits and to pinpoint the specific operational levers that would generate these financial benefits. Simply put, IBM measured both the specific financial improvements of its e-engineering projects as well as the means to change its work processes to achieve these financial benefits.

In addition, financial executives should note that IBM was willing to combine a number of different technologies to achieve business benefits. For example, IBM used procurement cards, a data warehouse, and the Internet as different means to achieve different, but related, business objectives.

BEST PRACTICES

The CCO and IBM cases suggest that e-commerce can substantially benefit the operations of many firms. Here are some things that executives can do to realize that benefit.

1 **Go online.** If executives in a company have not yet learned how to use the Internet, this should be the first step. The company's chief information officer should arrange for the CEO to gain access to the Internet with a high-speed connection. This connection should enable the CEO to discover for himself or herself some of the benefits of the Internet. Such benefits could include using e-mail to communicate with colleagues worldwide, following investments, purchasing airline tickets, and purchasing books. Once CEOs have found personal value in using the Web, they will be more inclined to see how it can help the company.

2 **Start with strategy.** The Internet can change the way a company works. For example, it could be an alternative sales channel or could leverage the customer service operation. The important point is that the Internet creates the opportunity to change the business so that customers will get a better value proposition. Using the Internet simply to publish an existing set of product brochures does not capture its full potential to enhance the firm's competitive position.

3 **Set an objective.** CEOs should pick a measurable objective and a deadline by which to achieve it. The goal might be a 20% reduction in the cost of handling a customer service transaction, to be achieved within 12 months. Or the goal might be to generate 20% of corporate sales over the Web within two years. Without a destination, any road is equally ineffective.

4 **Get different functions to work together**. Harnessing the power of the Web involves making fundamental changes in the way the company works. The change can happen only if the CEO drives the different functions to work together to achieve the objective. These internal partnerships should include a close working relationship between the IT department and the business managers. CEOs should make it clear that compensation will be linked to achieving the goal.

5 **Experiment and learn**. Looking at how other companies are using the Web is often a good way to get ideas. It is also essential that a company look at its new Web site from the perspective of customers. One large company developed a site that was organized around the company's organizational structure. The problem was that customers did not know how the company was organized, so the site was difficult to navigate. The only way to learn all the lessons is to experiment and to get feedback.

The Global Dimension

Globalization and technology have evolved together over the last couple of decades. This chapter highlights this co-evolution, providing a roadmap for managers. This chapter includes:

» an essay on the co-evolution of globalization and technology;
» key issues for management of globalization and technology; and
» best practices for harnessing globalization and technology to strengthen a firm's competitive position.

The term "globalization" is controversial. Some view it as a process that is an inevitable key to future world economic development. Others regard it with fear, believing that it increases inequality within and between nations, threatens employment and living standards, and limits social progress. This discussion offers an overview of some aspects of globalization and discusses the relationship between technological innovation and globalization – concluding with a discussion of best practices of technology and globalization.

Globalization offers opportunities for worldwide development but it is not progressing evenly. Some countries are becoming integrated into the global economy more quickly than others. Countries that have been able to integrate are seeing faster growth and reduced poverty. Globalization-oriented policies brought greater prosperity to much of East Asia, transforming it from the poor area of the world it was 40 years ago. As living standards have risen, it has become possible to make progress on democracy and economic issues such as the environment and work standards.

By contrast, in the 1970s and 1980s when many countries in Latin America and Africa pursued inward-oriented policies, their economies stagnated or declined, poverty increased and high inflation became common. In many cases, especially Africa, adverse external developments made the problems worse. As these regions changed their policies, their incomes began to rise. An important transformation is underway. Encouraging this trend, not reversing it, is the best course for promoting growth, development and poverty reduction.

The crises in the emerging markets in the 1990s made it quite evident that the opportunities of globalization do not come without risks, including those arising from volatile capital movements and the risks of social, economic, and environmental degradation created by poverty. This is not a reason to reverse direction, but rather a chance for all concerned – in developing countries, in the advanced countries, and of course investors – to embrace policy changes to build strong economies and a stronger world financial system that will produce more rapid growth and ensure that poverty is reduced.

Economic globalization is a historical process, the result of human innovation and technological progress. The term refers to the increasing integration of economies around the world, particularly through trade and financial flows. It sometimes also refers to the movement of people (labor) and knowledge (technology) across international borders.

At its most basic, there is nothing mysterious about globalization. The term has come into common usage since the 1980s, reflecting technological advances that have made it easier and quicker to complete international transactions – both trade and financial flows. It refers to an extension beyond national borders of the same market forces that have operated for centuries at all levels of human economic activity – village markets, urban industries, or financial centers.

Markets promote efficiency through competition and the division of labor – the specialization that allows people and economies to focus on what they do best. Global markets offer greater opportunity for people to access more and larger markets around the world. It means that they can have access to more capital flows, technology, cheaper imports, and larger export markets. But markets do not necessarily ensure that the benefits of increased efficiency are shared by all. Countries must be prepared to embrace the policies needed, and in the case of the poorest countries may need the support of the international community as they do so.

Globalization is not just a recent phenomenon. Some analysts have argued that the world economy was just as globalized 100 years ago as it is today. But today commerce and financial services are far more developed than they were at that time. The most striking aspect of this has been the integration of financial markets made possible by modern electronic communication.

The twentieth century saw economic growth, with global per capita GDP increasing almost five-fold. But this growth was not steady: the strongest expansion came during the second half of the century, a period of rapid trade expansion accompanied by trade – and typically somewhat later, financial – liberalization.

The story of the twentieth century was one of remarkable average income growth, but it is also quite obvious that the progress was not evenly dispersed. The gaps between rich and poor countries, and rich and poor people within countries, have grown. The richest quarter of the world's population saw its per capita GDP increase nearly six-fold during the century, while the poorest quarter experienced less than a three-fold increase. Income inequality has clearly increased.

Globalization means that world trade and financial markets are becoming more integrated. In some countries, especially in Asia, per capita incomes have been moving quickly since 1970 toward levels in the industrial countries. A larger number of developing countries have made only slow progress or have lost ground. In particular, per capita incomes in Africa have declined relative to the industrial countries and in some countries have declined in absolute terms. The countries catching up are those where trade has grown strongly.

Consider four aspects of globalization:

» **Trade**. Developing countries as a whole have increased their share of world trade – from 19% in 1971 to 29% in 1999. But there is great variation among the major regions. For instance, the newly industrialized economies (NIEs) of Asia have done well, while Africa as a whole has fared poorly. The composition of what countries export is also important. The strongest rise by far has been in the export of manufactured goods. The share of primary commodities in world exports – items such as food and raw materials, that are often produced by the poorest countries – has declined.

» **Capital movements**. Private capital flows to developing countries sharply increased during much of the 1990s. The increase followed a particularly "dry" period in the 1980s; net official flows of development assistance have fallen significantly since the early 1980s; and the composition of private flows has changed. Direct foreign investment has become the most important category. Both portfolio investment and bank credit rose, but they have been more volatile, falling sharply in the wake of the financial crises of the late 1990s.

» **Movement of people**. Workers move from one country to another partly to find better employment opportunities. The numbers involved are still quite small, but in the period 1965–90, the proportion of labor forces round the world that was foreign-born increased by about one-half. Most migration occurs between developing countries. However, the flow of migrants to advanced economies is likely to provide a means through which global wages converge. There is also the potential for skills to be transferred back to the developing countries and for wages in those countries to rise.

» **Spread of knowledge (and technology)**. Information exchange is an integral, often overlooked, aspect of globalization. For instance, direct foreign investment brings not only an expansion of the physical capital stock, but also technical innovation. More generally, knowledge about production methods, management techniques, export markets and economic policies is available at very low cost, and it represents a highly valuable resource for the developing countries.

The succession of crises in the 1990s – Mexico, Thailand, Indonesia, Korea, Russia, and Brazil – suggested that financial crises are a direct and inevitable result of globalization.

Clearly the crises would not have developed as they did without exposure to global capital markets. But nor could these countries have achieved their impressive growth records without those financial flows.

These were complex crises, resulting from an interaction of shortcomings in national policy and the international financial system. Individual governments and the international community as a whole are taking steps to reduce the risk of such crises in future.

At the national level, even though several of the countries had impressive records of economic performance, they were not fully prepared to withstand the potential shocks that could come through the international markets. Macroeconomic stability, financial soundness, open economies, transparency, and good governance are all essential for countries participating in the global markets. Each of the countries came up short in one or more respects.

At the international level, several important lines of defense against crisis were breached. Investors did not appraise risks adequately. Regulators and supervisors in the major financial centers did not monitor developments sufficiently closely, and not enough information was available about some international investors, notably offshore financial institutions. The result was that markets were prone to "herd behavior" – sudden shifts of investor sentiment and the rapid movement of capital, especially short-term finance, into and out of countries.

The international community is responding to the global dimensions of the crisis through a continuing effort to strengthen the architecture of the international monetary and financial system. The broad aim is for markets to operate with more transparency, equity, and efficiency.

As globalization has progressed, living conditions (particularly when measured by broader indicators of well-being) have improved significantly in virtually all countries. However, the strongest gains have been made by the advanced countries and only some of the developing countries. Technology has played an important role in encouraging globalization by facilitating communication among people around the world and accelerating the movement of goods globally. Technology companies have also changed the way they manage their operations as a result of globalization. For example, many technology companies outsource activities such as manufacturing or software development to regions of the world where these activities can be performed more cost-effectively and with high quality.

The trends in globalization raise significant issues regarding the management of innovation.

» Should all innovation be performed centrally or is it more useful to match up innovating employees with the locations where the products resulting from their efforts will be sold?

» Is it better to create mixed teams of innovators from different countries or do teams within the same country operate more effectively?

» Are there specific countries that have the highest concentration of expert innovators in specific technologies? If so, how can a firm best manage its hiring and retention policies to attract the best people within the most critical areas of technology?

» How can innovations developed in one or two countries be most profitably introduced into other geographic markets?

» What kinds of technology and training must a firm deploy in order to maximize the productivity of its innovating employees?

These issues have significant implications for general managers.

» Managers need to consider which activities they perform at a world class level.

» Managers should seek out partners who can perform activities which their firms do not perform at a world class level.

» Managers must assess whether the costs of co-ordinating business relationships with such partners are lower than the benefits from outsourcing.

» Managers must recognize that their customers and suppliers are expanding globally and therefore the companies must invest in technology to enhance global co-ordination.

» Managers must also invest in training people to work globally, including the development of an understanding of cultural differences and similarities.

Best practices for globalization and the management of technology include the following.

1 **Analyze the firm's value chain.** For many firms competing in different market segments, it is likely that the firm will need to create distinct value chains for each of the distinct markets in which it competes. Analyzing the firm's value chain implies developing a detailed understanding of the activities that a firm performs to create value for its customers. To be useful in the context of globalization and technology, such a value chain analysis should entail a detailed mapping of processes, assignment of costs to each activity, and an analysis of how well customers perceive the firm performs each activity.

2 **Assess which activities are world class and which are not.** Based on the analysis in step one, the firm should identify a set of competitors around the globe and perform a similar analysis of competitors' value chains. Based on this analysis, the firm should be able to assess which activities it performs on a world class level and which it does not.

3 **Find world class suppliers of the non-world class activities.** Using the results of this analysis, the firm should consider seeking out partners who perform at a world class level the activities where the firm is relatively weak. The result of this analysis should be a list of several firms around the world to which the firm could outsource selected activities.

4 **Analyze the costs of co-ordinating with these suppliers and the incremental benefits.** Next, the firm should analyze the costs of co-ordinating with these potential suppliers of outsourcing services – including the management costs, costs of communication and co-ordination, cost of switching over the performance of the activity, and initial and ongoing fees. The firm should then analyze the benefits of outsourcing to

the supplier, including reduced costs, and a higher level of performance of the activity that might be reflected in greater market share and/or higher prices. If the benefits of outsourcing appear to exceed the costs, then the firm should send out requests for quotation (RFQs) to potential suppliers and select the firm with the best proposal and references.

5 **Include service level agreements (SLAs) in outsourcing contracts.** In negotiating with potential suppliers, the firm should make clear the specific performance measures that will be used to assess the outsourcer's performance. These performance measures should be reflected in the outsourcing contracts as SLAs that are agreed on by the firm and its outsourcer before the relationship is formalized.

6 **Link incentives to performance relative to SLAs in outsourcing contracts.** Furthermore, firms should link incentives to performance on the SLAs. Simply put, if the outsourcer exceeds the performance levels specified in the SLAs, the firm should pay a bonus to the outsourcer. If the outsourcer falls short of the performance levels specified in the SLAs, the firm should withhold bonus payments. If the outsourcer consistently falls far short of the SLA performance levels, the firm should move to cancel the contract and find a better performing outsourcer.

7 **Invest in technology and training to facilitate global co-ordination.** Finally, firms should recognize that operating globally implies that the firm will need to invest in technology to facilitate global operations. Such technology may include global Virtual Private Networks, videoconferencing equipment, and global databases. Furthermore, firms must recognize that operating globally demands that all workers receive training that enables the workers to work more effectively with individuals from different cultures.

The State of the Art

Management of innovation is a topic that continues to evolve, so what are today's hot topics? This chapter explores the following topics:

» key technological changes influencing the structure of industries and the management of innovation;
» significant issues that these changes create for managers, technologists, and employees; and
» implications of these challenges for managers, investors, workers, and consumers.

Companies that participate in technology-intensive industries are exposed to a powerful set of industry forces that enhance the challenge of maintaining high levels of profitability.

» **The frequency with which price/performance-enhancing new products are introduced has increased dramatically**. In semiconductors, for example, the price/performance ratio of CPUs, according to Moore's Law, has doubled every 18 months. This rapid acceleration of change forces competitors to either keep up the pace or risk falling behind and ultimately ceding markets to more aggressive competitors.

» **At the same time, industry-transforming technological shifts occur with startling rapidity**. IBM's position in the computer industry, buttressed by the central role of its proprietary mainframes, was substantially undermined when Microsoft took control of the operating system for the personal computer. Microsoft's position was then threatened by a concept advocated by Oracle and others of a $500 Internet Box that rapidly downloads information and office applications from the Internet. Ultimately, Microsoft adapted to this threat by introducing the concept of Web services that enabled customers to buy software on a subscription basis to work in a networked environment.

» **Furthermore, the traditional role of patents as a means of building a moat around intellectual property has substantially eroded**. Patents certainly play a role in the pharmaceutical industry, where investments in developing new products can reach as high as $500mn, thereby making a 17-year patent protection essential to recouping this investment. In virtually all other technology-based industries, however, by the time a patent has been approved, the state of the market may be several generations beyond the technology being patented. In other words, companies in technology-intensive industries are no longer able to rely on patents to maintain their leadership position. They are much better off investing in a work environment that successfully attracts and retains scientists and engineers who repeatedly introduce profitable new products to the marketplace ahead of their competitors.

» **In many technology-based industries, including computer hardware, telecommunications, and software, companies that**

create and control an industry standard enjoy market positions that result in very high profitability. A classic example of this is Microsoft's establishment of MS-DOS and Windows as the industry standard operating system. Working with Intel and other developers, Microsoft leveraged its position in operating systems to build a profitable position in a range of software products. Given the low entry barriers into the software industry, in particular, a large number of small companies can develop software to solve specific problems. Corporate customers need to minimize the risk of purchasing software from a vendor who may not be able to adapt to their changing needs and who may not be able to offer support for and compatibility with their existing systems. In these markets, the emergence of a standard that is perceived as minimizing these risks confers tremendous market power on its creator(s).

» **The pressures on existing firms to keep pace with these changes has resulted in record levels of mergers and acquisitions**. Technology executives are increasingly realizing that the risk of being left out of an industry-transforming technology is substantially greater than the cost of acquiring a company that has established leadership in that technology. Several years ago, AT&T's $11.5bn acquisition of McCaw Cellular was driven by the realization that building a national cellular network would be much more time-consuming and costly than buying the company. Similarly, Cisco Systems' $4bn purchase of StrataCom resulted from a similar calculation for ATM (Asynchronous Transfer Mode – a relatively fast, though expensive, data communications standard).

» **In many technology-based industries, the "horizontal negotiating leverage" has shifted from technology suppliers to technology consumers**. An essential element of the success of HP and Digital, for example, was that engineers designed products for themselves. Because these companies created an environment that attracted and retained the best engineers, other engineers who bought these products were happy to have their product needs dictated to them. As a result of a shift to open operating systems, the creation of more efficient channels of distribution, and the growing importance of selling computers to consumer markets, the "next bench" paradigm was fundamentally altered. More specifically, these trends created an opportunity for buyers to compare the products of a wider array of vendors and to use their volume purchases to force a dramatic reduction in overall product cost of purchase and use while demanding steady improvements in product performance. While HP responded effectively to this change, particularly in laser printers, Digital's performance lagged HP, partially as a result of its inability to respond to changing customer needs. This shift has also influenced the pharmaceutical industry, as exemplified by Merck's $6bn purchase of Medco, a high volume consumer of pharmaceutical products for managed care programs.

» **Finally, companies in technology-intensive industries continuously re-evaluate their core technologies**. This process has led to dramatic growth in strategic alliances among companies seeking to limit the risks associated with participating in new markets. For example, HP negotiated a strategic alliance with Intel to develop a 64-bit CPU that HP was unwilling to finance itself. These alliances, however, are inherently unstable, creating significant management challenges as companies find themselves simultaneously co-operating and competing with each other in different markets. For example, Microsoft agreed to allow America Online to establish itself on its Windows 95 operating system in exchange for America Online's agreement to use Microsoft Internet Explorer, a World Wide Web browser. In this deal, Microsoft was simultaneously trying to increase the market penetration of its Web browser, while helping the competition for its Microsoft Network online information service.

ISSUES FOR CEOS, CHIEF TECHNOLOGY OFFICERS AND OTHERS

These competitive challenges have unique implications for CEOs, chief technology officers, division managers, product managers and engineers.

CEO Issues

CEOs in technology-intensive industries may need to address issues such as: how do the changes in my industry affect the attractiveness of the markets in which we compete? How do these changes influence our competitive position in these markets? Should we be selling/outsourcing some of our businesses or functions? Are there important technologies that we should acquire or license, rather than build internally? What impact do these changes have on the value of our assets, including our research portfolio? In light of these changes, are our managers and other employees the right individuals to achieve our business objectives? Are we working on the right product development projects? Do our financial and other incentives create the right environment to reinforce the importance of achieving these objectives?

Chief technology officer issues

CTOs may need to address issues such as: do we have the right balance between "technology" and "business" in our research organization? How good are we at introducing profitable new products to the market ahead of our competitors? What are our "core technologies" and are we maximizing their value? What are our "non-core technologies" and are we managing them to balance efficiency and access? Are we attracting and retaining the best scientists and engineers and are we maximizing their productivity? Do we understand the value of our research portfolio and are we taking a systematic approach to reallocating people and capital from less valuable to the most valuable projects?

Division manager issues

Division managers have been forced to deal with a set of issues that are similar to those facing CEOs, only on a smaller scale. In particular, division managers must also question the extent to which they should look for ways to share capabilities with other divisions in order to enhance the company's overall performance. At the same time, division managers may be concerned both for themselves, and for division employees, that participation in such cross-divisional projects may not be appropriately rewarded by corporate incentive systems.

Product manager issues

Product managers may need to deal with issues such as: to what extent will the organization recognize the enhanced importance of managing cross-functional teams? In particular, will the organization create the kinds of financial and other incentives necessary to facilitate the co-ordination of engineering, manufacturing, marketing, sales and finance to introduce profitable new products ahead of competitors?

Engineer issues

Engineers may be faced with issues such as: how will these competitive challenges affect the status of engineering? Whereas engineering traditionally enjoyed a position at the top of the functional hierarchy, will it now be required to share high status with other functions, possibly manufacturing and marketing staff? Will engineers continue to have the opportunity to advance their professional interests and push the state-of-the-art or will the work be focused exclusively on applying less advanced technology for more immediately marketable products? Will the company reward engineering as its role becomes more commercial or will engineers seek employment in other organizations where staying on the cutting edge of technology is more highly valued?

What lessons will participants in the economy take from technology leaders in order to address these challenges?

GENERAL BUSINESS LANDSCAPE

Industries can be categorized by the basic elements on which they depend for their success. Arrayed in evolutionary sequence, there are four such elements: natural resources, manufacturing, distribution, and smart people. Over the last 200 years, the "magic wand" of wealth creation has been passed from the people who control the natural resources to the people who control the smart people.

Obviously, there continue to be huge American industries that depend on all four of these elements, in a variety of combinations. However, the industries that set the pace for the rest of the economy are the ones where the most new wealth is being created. And the most new wealth is being created by the technology leaders.

As pace setters, the management principles that technology leaders follow are likely to cascade throughout the rest of the economy. It is unlikely that these principles magically embed themselves in every American company. It is more likely that these principles will spread from the technology leaders to some early-adopter companies. From these early-adopter companies, these principles may spread to the rest of American business.

It is impossible to predict which industries and which companies will be the early-adopters or how these principles will spread beyond the early-adopters. One possible scenario is that the principles spread backwards through the evolutionary sequence of basic elements. In other words, other high-tech companies might adopt the principles first. Then distribution-based industries like financial services and retailing, big customers of the technology companies, would adopt the principles. From there, the principles might spread to manufacturing-based industries like automobiles and chemicals. Finally, they might be adopted by the natural resources companies.

Having described how these principles might spread throughout the economy, how will they change the general business landscape? First, organizations will become less bureaucratic and more flexible. Second, companies will move in and out of markets more quickly. Third, big and small businesses will need to learn how to work together more effectively.

Large organizations will *dismantle hierarchy*. They will push real decision-making authority to the people who deal with customers. Everybody in the organization will be evaluated and paid based on objective feedback from the marketplace. They will have a real stake in the success of their company. As a result, organizations will adapt to change more rapidly than ever.

Large organizations will *move in and out of markets* more quickly. As companies get better at learning, they will recognize that opportunities for profit in specific markets don't last forever. Companies will become more like arbitrageurs. They will get better at sniffing out profit opportunities and assembling the pieces that they need to exploit them. Once the profit has been earned, they will move on.

To make this happen, large and small organizations will need to *learn how to work together*. The large organizations will compete for the new ideas generated by the small companies. The small companies will need the large company's capital, manufacturing, and distribution. At the point of connection, then, large and small companies will need to become more alike in order to work together effectively. The success rate for these business alliances will need to increase dramatically.

How will these changes to the general business landscape affect managers, workers, consumers, and financiers?

MANAGERS

Technology leaders will have an impact on managers in four important ways. First, technology leaders will change the way companies manage people. Second, technology leaders will change the attitude towards organizational learning. Third, technology leaders will transform the skills required to be a CEO. Finally, the emergence of the Internet is likely to demand a new form of management I call e-management.

One of the reasons that technology leaders succeed is that they attract the smartest *people*. This simple idea is extremely powerful. In the past, companies won by getting a lock on scarce resources like gold, oil, or gas. In many technology-based industries today, the physical component of the product is a few grains of sand. What separates the winners from the losers is the intellectual content of the product. This intellectual content comes from people. It therefore follows that the most successful companies will be the ones that get the people who can put the best intellectual content into their products. As we saw in studying Microsoft, there is a big difference in productivity between the very smartest programmer and the others.

As technology leaders grow in wealth, this dynamic will spread throughout the economy. In industry after industry, the importance of brain power will grow. Companies that attract and retain the smartest people will prosper. Companies that cling to what worked in the past will rapidly fade away. So, as a result of what technology leaders do, managers will need to create work environments that win the competition for the smartest people.

Second, technology leaders will change managers' attitudes towards *organizational learning*. Technology leaders will use learning to get further and further ahead. They will keep their smartest people plugged in to changes in customer needs, technologies and competitor strategies. Nothing will be able to stop these companies from getting more and more competitive. As they extend their reach into the economy, their ability to learn will create so much wealth that other companies will try to imitate it. So, if you want to be on the right side of the power curve, learn how to learn.

Third, technology leaders are making it *impossible for managers to be ignorant about technology*. The wealth of technology leaders will fuel their continued penetration into all aspects of business. As a result, managers will no longer be able to hide behind a chief information or chief technology officer. In the future, managers will be selected based on their ability to use technology to create customer value. Managers who do not understand technology will fall behind fast. So, if you are an aspiring manager, you need to get comfortable with technology.

Fourth, the Internet is likely to create the need for a new form of management called e-management, which to me means the ability to generate consistently outstanding financial results in a very turbulent world. E-management shares four features of traditional management while presenting a set of four unique challenges.

The shared characteristics of traditional and e-management include the following.

» **The performance imperative**. The need to generate consistently outstanding financial performance (as measured by earnings growth, return on equity, and stock price performance) is just as strong in the traditional world as in the e-world. Between 1995 and 2000 investors rewarded fast growing dot-coms that lost money. Since the April 2000 crash, investors punished firms that could not generate outstanding financial performance and rewarded those who could.

» **Attracting and motivating top people**. An enduring reality of management is that the winning firms are the ones that can attract the best people and motivate them to do the right things. The meaning of these terms (e.g., best people and right things) is likely to be very different for different industries; however, the need for effective managers to figure out who the best people are and how to motivate them well is likely to be critical, whether in a traditional company or an e-company.

» **What's measured gets done**. An important way to attract and motivate the best people is to create an effective performance measurement system that makes it clear to people how their activities are linked to outstanding financial performance. While this concept sounds simple, its effective execution makes the difference between a well-managed company and its peers. Furthermore, linking performance measurement to incentives is a critical component of getting people to do the right things. If performers are rewarded and non-performers are punished, then people in the organization will do what gets rewarded. The managerial imperative to create and use such performance systems is critical in traditional and e-companies.

» **Breeding the next generation of management is job 1**. While some e-companies were built to flip, the long-term leaders recognize that creating the next generation of leadership is the most important responsibility of the CEO. While few e-companies have been tested in this area, there are many that may end up emulating Jack Welch, who used a combination of astute hiring, job rotations, mentoring, and training to breed a very deep bench at GE.

While e-management shares these characteristics with traditional management, e-management also presents unique challenges.

» **Need for mastery of the virtual and physical worlds**. The best e-managers recognize that customers will give more of their business to companies that offer more value for less money. Winning e-managers know that delivering a superior value proposition means sustaining world class capabilities in both the virtual and physical worlds. Simply put, e-management demands a sort of managerial ambidexterity which is rare as it is valuable. This managerial ambidexterity also demands the ability to link capabilities in the virtual and physical worlds in such a seamless manner that customers will only notice how much better their experience is with the e-managed firm.

» **Skill at positioning the firm within a network of industries**. E-management also demands the ability to see how the firm fits into a broader system of value creation. Simply put, e-management is different because practicing e-management well requires the e-engineering of broad business ecosystems. For example, Microsoft is attempting through its Hailstorm set of Net services to streamline the interactions among suppliers, customers, and customers' customers. Such systemic e-engineering demands the ability to enhance the value in not just a few business relationships but an entire system of such relationships.

» **Ability to filter signal from noise**. E-management demands the ability to be connected to thousands of inputs about specific changes among many industry participants such as suppliers, customers, employees, competitors, media, and shareholders. Effective e-management requires the ability to monitor developments that can change with unusually high frequency. However, given the huge number and frequency of these inputs, it is also essential that e-managers are able to distinguish between the few meaningful inputs and the many inputs that have limited significance for the positioning of the firm. The number of e-managers who can filter these inputs effectively is very small – an elite club whose skills are well rewarded.

» **Ability to sustain organizational change**. The e-world forces organizations to adapt well to change. With stunning swiftness a leading firm can lose its market position. For example, Cisco Systems went from dominating the router market to giving up 38% of that market to an upstart, Juniper Networks, in a mere 24 months. Effective e-managers monitor changes in their markets and adapt rapidly to stay ahead of these changes.

WORKERS

These changes will bifurcate the workforce. There will be a very small number of workers who make a tremendous difference to society. And there will be the vast majority of workers who live comfortably but unremarkably.

The most successful companies will compete for the services of an elite group of smart, technically savvy, highly energetic workers. These smart people will enjoy interesting careers and become quite wealthy.

The rest of the workforce will make enough money to live comfortably. They will enjoy a better lifestyle because they will use home computers linked to corporate networks as a means of balancing their work and personal lives. Most workers will pay a price for this. Their careers will be more mundane and their opportunities for wealth will be relatively limited.

Worker training will become more important than it is now. Schools will need to give people the skills that companies need in their workers. Elite colleges and universities will need to develop courses that give workers the technical and organizational skills that businesses require of their elite core. Public schools will need to provide the rest of the workforce with a more solid grounding in reading, mathematics, and computers.

CONSUMERS

Technology leaders will continue to create products that improve the lives of consumers. On the other hand, some technology companies will churn out many products that consumers don't want. Of course, the market will take care of these companies over time.

Technology leaders have conditioned consumers to expect more "bang for the buck." It is likely that this trend will continue as long as more processing power can be crammed onto semiconductors at a lower and lower unit cost. At some point, however, there may be a huge time lag between greater CPU price/performance and the ability to develop applications that customers are willing to pay for.

This gap is beginning to be felt by Intel as it wonders whether new uses can be found for all the powerful CPUs that can be churned out by semiconductor fabrication plants whose cost is rapidly growing from $2bn to $10bn a copy. With these cost increases, the number of units that must be sold to make a profit on the incremental fab goes up exponentially. Companies like Intel must invest in developing large markets that can consume the processing power that they produce. Otherwise, the entire industry, as it is currently configured, could collapse.

Consumers will probably continue to have a choice of new products that give them greater value. At some point, the consumer market for technology products, such as home computers, will reach saturation. When this occurs, consumers could experience diminishing returns to "upgrading." Simply put, if a new product or a new version does not give the consumer enough additional value to justify spending the extra money, most consumers will stick with what they have. As long as technology leaders can continue to create enough additional value to get consumers to upgrade, this problem can be deferred and growth can continue.

FINANCIERS

Technology leaders will have a big impact on financiers as well. First, technology leaders will compete directly with venture capitalists.

Second, they will create tremendous wealth for shareholders, so portfolio managers will want to own their stocks. Third, they will create technology that transforms the process of raising and investing capital.

Venture capital

Many technology leaders have created their own venture capital arms. Certainly these companies have access to capital as a result of their enormous market valuations. In addition, they have two other critical ingredients: understanding of technology and markets, and managerial talent. What this means is that the returns that venture capitalists can earn are likely to diminish as more competitors chase a fairly limited pool of good deals.

Of course, this reversion towards the mean could be prevented if venture capitalists find new ways to compete. One such model could be found at Kleiner Perkins. KPCB has invested in companies that potentially "own" critical components of the Internet business model. In other words, as the Internet becomes a way to make money, Kleiner Perkins will own equity in the most valuable pieces.

What is potentially unique here is that the firm encourages different companies that it owns to do business with each other. As a result, it is possible that more value will be created than could have been generated by a passive investor who simply bought and held shares in the companies.

One thing is certain, venture capitalists will face more competition for good deals, and will therefore need to come up with new ideas for how to compete in order to continue to earn above average returns. Technology leaders changed their fundamental approach to accessing new technology by getting into the venture capital business. Their entry into the market will force incumbents to change their fundamental business processes as well.

Investment opportunities

The 20 companies that were analyzed here generated shareholder wealth at over four-and-a-half times the market rate during the first half of the 1990s. Put another way, if an investor had purchased stock in the 20 technology leaders in 1990, their investment would have grown at a compound annual rate of over 180%.

It is unlikely that an investment in the same portfolio of stocks will produce similar results in the future. Nevertheless, it is possible that investors can learn something from what made these companies do so well. Part of the answer has to do with buying the stock before the rest of the market figures out how valuable it is.

Technology leaders share five characteristics that could be useful leading indicators for a diligent investor. First, the company should participate in a market that is growing very fast. Second, it should be led by a CEO who combines a deep understanding of technology with tremendous business savvy. Third, it should have a product with an outstanding reputation among early-adopters and industry experts. Fourth, it should have a reputation among top engineers and scientists as being a great place to work. Fifth, the company should be profitable and have a balance sheet with lots of cash and minimal debt. Since the first four of these criteria require some digging to get the answers, they could provide an advantage to a diligent investor.

Investment technology

Technology leaders will create technology that changes the nature of capital markets. Just as technology companies succeed by hiring the smartest engineers, so do investment firms succeed by hiring the smartest financiers. In fact, over the last decade, the investment houses have been able to hire many of the same math and science PhD graduates that the high-tech companies wanted to hire.

The competition among securities valuation models is likely to affect investor returns and traders' incomes. Since the mid-1980s, financiers have developed models that identify difficult to detect patterns in the financial markets. These patterns create opportunities to execute trades that take advantage of tiny and very short-lived mis-pricing of securities. At the core of these sophisticated models is a very high powered computer, huge volumes of accurate and timely securities price information, and a small number of very smart mathematicians and scientists who analyze the data to identify these investment opportunities.

As the power of the technology increases, these models will have much shorter half-lives during which they generate high investor returns. As a result, the competition will continue on the basis of who has the smartest people, who has the best data, and who has the most powerful tools for analyzing the data to identify the investment opportunities.

Of course, technology will also reduce transaction costs for the more mundane parts of the capital markets. For example, at some point the financial advantages of an all-electronic stock trading system will overwhelm the political power of the specialists who control today's hybrid system. Fundamental analysis and real-time securities price information will be available to all market participants at a nominal price. Securities custody and accounting functions will be performed with tremendous efficiency. These process improvements will drive down transaction costs and reduce information asymmetries, making the capital markets much more efficient.

Technology leaders will continue to make the world a better place. The business landscape will become more efficient as technology leaders find new ways to create greater customer value at a lower cost. Managers will compete for the smartest workers and create work environments that stress learning and adaptation. Workers will have greater freedom and responsibility in directing their careers. Consumers will have a broad range of products that deliver more bang for their buck. And financiers will develop new ways to raise capital efficiently and invest it at high rates of return.

In Practice: Case Studies in Technology Leadership

What does it take to profit from successive waves of technology? This chapter provides the answer by presenting case studies of global technology leaders including:

» Hewlett-Packard;
» EMC;
» Schlumberger;
» Microsoft; and
» Gillette.

Technology leaders manage their people and technology to create products that customers eagerly buy. Technology leaders do this by choosing a boundaryless approach to product development. This approach works because it opens clogged communication channels.

Technology leaders make better products because they mix the ideas of different participants. They identify problems early, before too much money has been spent. By looking at design problems from different perspectives they get ideas that would not have emerged from any individual function working by itself. And because they don't leave out important participants, they are not blindsided at the last minute.

Technology leaders approach product development with intellectual humility. As a result, technology leaders open their minds to changes in customer needs, technologies, and competitive behavior.

HEWLETT-PACKARD'S INKJET

The case of HP's development of its inkjet technology illustrates this mindset. HP capitalized on its internally developed inkjet technology to take PC printer market leadership from Epson, the dominant dot matrix printer vendor. Between 1988 and 1995, overall inkjet unit volume rose from 0 to almost 8 million units while dot matrix unit volume dropped from 6 million to 3 million units.

An HP engineer discovered inkjet printing in a converted janitor's closet in its Vancouver, WA office. In 1979, an HP scientist noticed drops of liquid splattered over his lab bench. He had been charging a thin metal film with electricity. When the metal grew hot, liquid trapped underneath began to boil and spurted out. This discovery evolved into the "thermal" inkjet. HP's executive in charge, Richard Hackborn, recognized that inkjet technology had several advantages over laser printers for the mass market: it was less expensive, more easily adaptable for color printing, and had not been perfected by competitors.

HP's first inkjet printer, introduced in 1984, was not a success. It required special paper and it printed only 96 dots per inch (compared to 600 dots in 1995). While Epson, a vendor of dot matrix printers, thought that HP's first product was an embarrassment, HP saw the inkjet technology as the basis for satisfying a mass market that would demand higher-quality printouts of text, graphics and photographs.

Hackborn chose to "learn from the Japanese" by investing heavily in its low cost inkjet technology, building it into a family of products that could fill retail shelves.

Canon, which had patented early inkjet designs and then shared them with HP, chose a complex implementation that would take many years to develop. Epson's US executives tried unsuccessfully to convince Japanese headquarters that Epson should introduce a high-quality printer to meet the demands of low budget US PC users. Because of Epson's large dot matrix revenue base, profits, and technological history, Epson declined to develop its expensive inkjet technology variant.

Meanwhile, HP engineers filed several patents on its own inkjet technology and began a process of continual improvement to solve the inkjet's problems. HP developed print heads that could generate 300 dots per inch and made inks that would stay liquid in the cartridge but dry instantly on plain paper.

In 1988, HP introduced the Deskjet, the first version of the plain-paper copier that ultimately took share from the Japanese products. Although HP had no inkjet rivals at the time, the product was not meeting its sales goals in 1989. The inkjet was competing with HP's more costly laser printers. Inkjet sales were too low to support its high research and manufacturing costs. Due to HP's policy of requiring its divisions to be financially self-supporting, the inkjet division needed new markets to avert a financial crisis.

In the autumn of 1989, a group of engineers and managers held a two-day retreat at Mount Hood. While reviewing market share charts, HP realized that it had been targeting the wrong enemy. Instead of positioning the inkjet as a low cost alternative to HP's laser printers, the managers decided to attack the Japanese-dominated dot matrix market. Dot matrix had poor print quality and color. Furthermore, Epson, the dot matrix leader, had no competitive inkjet and was distracted by an expensive and failing effort to sell a PC.

HP attacked Epson beginning with an in depth analysis of its market share, marketing strategies, public financial data, loyal customers, and top managers. In addition, HP engineers reverse engineered Epson printers to search for design and manufacturing ideas. HP's analysis of Epson generated useful insights. HP discovered that Epson marketers convinced stores to put printers in the most prominent locations. HP also learned that Epson used price cuts to defend itself from challengers. HP found out that consumers liked Epson reliability. Finally, HP found out that Epson printers were designed to be easy to manufacture.

HP responded by demanding that stores put its printers next to Epson's. HP also tripled its warranty. And HP redesigned its printers for ease of manufacturing. In its competitor analysis, HP had also learned that Epson could create a very broad product line by making slight variations in the same basic platform. HP, on the other hand, had a history of creating an entirely new platform for each new product version.

Engineers were very upset at the suggestion to make minor modifications to the existing platform. They reluctantly agreed, however, only after the product manager forced engineers to conduct a telephone poll of customers that showed that customers wanted to buy a product that was a slight variation of HP's existing platform. By remaining with this platform, HP was able to introduce a product to market far earlier than its competitors for the now rapidly growing color printer market.

When Tandy opened its stores in 1991, it told suppliers to make inkjets available to meet what it anticipated to be very strong demand. Only HP had product available. When Japanese printer makers that had been investing in inkjet research tried to enter the market, they found that HP had locked up many important patents. Citizens Watch Company, for example, found that HP had 50 patents covering how ink travels through the head. NEC found that years went by during which it was unable to replicate HP's technology, enabling HP to gain an even greater lead over its competitors.

By the time Canon introduced the first credible competition, HP had already sold millions of its printers and had thousands of outlets for its replacement cartridges. HP used its experience to make continuous improvements in manufacturing. As a result, by 1994 the Deskjet cost half its 1988 level in constant dollars.

When Canon was about to introduce a color inkjet printer in 1993, HP cut the price of its own version before Canon reached the market. The black and white printer, priced at $995 in 1988, listed for $365 in 1994. When NEC tried to introduce an inexpensive monochrome inkjet printer, HP launched an improved color version and cut the price of its best-selling black-and-white model by 40% over six months.

HP's willingness to compete with its prior versions enabled it to grow revenues and to dominate increasingly value-conscious segments of its market while blocking the entry of new competitors. Between 1984 and 1994, for example, HP's share of the US printer market grew from 2% to 55%.

The HP inkjet case demonstrates how an established firm can reinvent itself. The concept of the value triangle suggests how critical it is to create superior customer value in order to launch a truly successful innovation.

VALUE TRIANGLE ILLUSTRATED: VIDEO-ON-DEMAND AND EMC CORPORATION CASES

The history of video-on-demand and interactive television services illustrates how much money and effort can be devoted to technology in search of a market. In early 1994, many regional telecommunications and cable television companies announced strategic alliances to take advantage of the "coming boom" in video-on-demand services. Interactive TV trials were announced with great fanfare in regional markets throughout the United States.

Behind the hype was the Baby Bells' fear that cable companies would use video-on-demand to get a foothold in the local telephone market. So their willingness to pursue these alliances sprang, in part, from a desire to keep cable companies from taking their customers.

As of December 1996, none of these ventures had produced favorable returns. In that month, Bell Atlantic, Nynex, and Pacific Telesis Group took steps to pull the plug on Tele-TV. It was estimated that the companies had invested roughly $0.5bn over two years in this interactive television venture. Why did they pull out? Technical difficulties, rising costs, and vast changes in the market all contributed to their decision.

When the deal was announced, the participants thought that the Information Highway would be fiber-optic TV systems. Two years later, it had become clear that the Information Highway was the Internet. In addition, it turned out to be much more difficult and expensive than originally thought to build the fiber-optic TV system (the three companies had originally split a $300mn investment). In the interim, Congress passed telecommunications legislation that allowed the Baby

Bells to enter the $70bn long distance market. As a result, the three companies decided it would be better to close down the venture and try for a piece of the long distance market instead.

A 1995 Unisys study of business and residential customers suggested another problem with such interactive TV services: *customers didn't want them*. The Unisys survey indicated that the vast majority of residential customers simply want their basic phone service to work right. Customers asked for accurate bills, no breakdowns, one-call problem resolution and fraud protection. By contrast, only 16% said that services such as video-on-demand were very important to them.

Efforts by these telecommunications companies to introduce video-tex into the US market met a similar fate. In short, technology-driven products and services often consume tremendous capital resources without yielding a return.

Technology leaders avoid this common trap – by "connecting the corners of the value triangle." The first corner of the value triangle is the specific, ranked needs of target customers. The second corner is the attributes of the company's product. And the third corner is the firm's technologies and other capabilities.

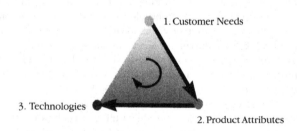

Fig. 7.1 The value triangle.

The key to the value triangle is the sequence that firms use to connect the corners. Technology leaders connect the corners in a clockwise direction (see Fig. 7.1). First they listen to their target customers to understand their needs, the first corner. They connect the first and second corners by choosing product attributes that meet these customer needs *better than competing products*. Finally, they connect the second and third corners by developing, or bringing in, the technologies and other capabilities required to realize these superior product attributes. Since the product attributes outperform the competition in meeting customer needs and the technology delivers these product attributes, it follows that the technology meets customer needs.

Peer companies, on the other hand, connect the corners in the counter-clockwise direction. First, engineers and scientists tinker with technologies that they find interesting, the third corner. Next, they loosely connect the second and third corners by building a prototype that uses the technology that they think could make a good product. Finally, they loosely connect the first and second corners by seeking out a business unit willing to see if some customers have any interest in the prototype.

Usually this sequence doesn't work. In the unusual case where it does work, the technology just happens to meet a customer need in a competitively unique way. This connection is made very infrequently when the corners of the value triangle are connected counter-clockwise.

If a company connects the corners in the clockwise direction, it wins. If it connects the dots in the counter-clockwise direction, it usually loses. The case of Tele-TV is a variant on the counter-clockwise model. The Baby Bells were afraid of losing their customers to the cable companies. They looked at what the cable companies were trying to do - upgrade their networks to handle telephone calls - and they invested in technology to support viewer ordering of movies on demand, that *they thought* would be better for customers.

The Baby Bells first studied the second corner, product attributes of competing products. They then went to the third corner, investing in technology and other capabilities, without ever touching the first corner - understanding customer needs. The assumption that companies know what customers want is the biggest impediment to market success.

Let's look at an example of what happens when a company connects the corners clockwise.

EMC Corporation is a technology leader whose 2000 sales totaled $9.4bn. Its return on equity between 1991 and 2000 averaged 23%, the top in its industry. During the same period, EMC Corporation's stock price increased 41,462%.

EMC Corporation took on IBM in the information storage and retrieval market and won. In 1990, IBM controlled 75% of the market, while EMC Corporation was not a player. By 1995, EMC Corporation had outmaneuvered IBM and others to take first place in this market.

EMC Corporation started in the early 1980s as a vendor of memory boards for minicomputers. In 1988, EMC Corporation hired Mike Ruettgers as EVP of Operations and Customer Service and promoted him to President and COO in 1989.

EMC Corporation's dramatic surge resulted from three crucial insights. First, EMC Corporation realized that mainframe storage customers wanted cheaper, faster, more reliable storage systems. Second, EMC Corporation understood that IBM, the market leader, was so caught up in its internal conflicts that it would be unable to meet these customer needs. Third, after introducing early products that met with some success, EMC Corporation developed a radical technology architecture that exceeded customer expectations.

There is abundant evidence that EMC Corporation gives its customers what they want. In 1993, 1995, and 1996 EMC Corporation was rated first in product quality, support and value for money over all other hardware vendors according to an independent survey of 530 sites by IBM Mainframe Users Information Exchange (IBEX). EMC Corporation beat off Hewlett-Packard, AT&T/NCR, Hitachi Data Systems, Storage Technology, Amdahl and others.

Consider how EMC Corporation helped one customer, IMS America, to compete more effectively. IMS America produces sales reports for pharmaceutical companies. In order to grow with its customers, IMS needed to help pharmaceutical companies to compete more effectively. To do this, IMS tailored its sales reports to analyze pharmaceutical sales data by distribution channel, geography and other market segments. Compared to the system that it replaced, EMC Corporation's product helped IMS to reduce by 25 to 50% the amount of time it takes to produce such sales reports. In addition, the EMC Corporation system reduced monthly downtime significantly.

EMC Corporation recognized that IBM would have a very hard time mounting a competitive response. EMC Corporation knew that

IBM used several different system architectures. As a result, it took longer for IBM to develop new products because different IBM groups were fighting for resources. In 1995, for example, IBM announced that it had canceled its previously announced plans to enhance the competitiveness of its product. IBM had intended to add to the RAID (Redundant Arrays of Inexpensive Disk) capacity of its 3990 Model 6 Controller, to keep pace with EMC Corporation. According to IBM, the plans were canceled due to "budgetary limitations and performance issues." This change in plans put IBM customers in the position of needing to add another controller, an expensive alternative, instead of simply adding drives, in order to increase storage capacity.

To exceed the requirements of its mainframe storage customers, EMC Corporation developed a single product architecture, MOSAIC:2000, that enables the company to introduce valuable products to its target market segments (mainframe, midrange, and open systems) ahead of its competitors. The design groups for EMC Corporation's largest product family share MOSAIC:2000 across products. As a result, innovations in one design group can be quickly transferred to the others. Furthermore, as new markets develop, EMC Corporation has a common platform that it can use to develop innovative solutions for storage management.

And at the core of EMC Corporation's disk storage products is Integrated Cached Array Technology (ICDA). This technology is the key to giving customers what they want: faster data retrieval from storage, leading to improved computer system performance. ICDA employs software to combine the high performance of cache memory technology with the high capacity and availability of arrays of small disks.

EMC Corporation won by connecting the corners of the value triangle clockwise. First, it understood what customers wanted. Second, it figured out what product attributes it would need to beat IBM. And finally, EMC Corporation built a technology architecture that enabled it to realize these superior product attributes. MOSAIC:2000 and ICDA technologies gave EMC Corporation the ability to provide customers faster, more reliable data retrieval at a lower cost. IBM, tied in knots by internal competition, was unable to compete in the marketplace. As a result, EMC Corporation went from nowhere to the number one slot in five years.

BUILDING CROSS-FUNCTIONAL TEAMS

Much has been written about the virtues of cross-functional teams. They are touted as a means to shorten time to market, to lower cost, and to increase market acceptance for new products. Many technology leaders have grappled successfully with the organizational challenges that are associated with making the transformation from a "relay race" approach to a cross-functional team approach. Hewlett-Packard and Schlumberger have successfully executed this transformation.

Hewlett-Packard

Before HP decided to create the laser printer and inkjet printer markets, the company had placed engineers at the top of its functional hierarchy. HP developed many of its products using what it called the "next bench" approach: engineers developed products for the engineer sitting next to them. With its move into the laser printer market, HP realized that Canon was the best vendor in the world for supplying laser printing technology. HP's CEO brought a team to Japan to observe Canon's operations and realized that in order for HP to succeed in this market, it would need to change its approach to product development. In particular, HP chose to elevate the role of manufacturing and marketing to a level equivalent to engineering. This new approach to product development was attempted at its Vancouver facility and due to its success, it became a model that other HP divisions emulated.

Schlumberger

Schlumberger, a leader in the oil services business, executed a similar transformation of its product development process.

Seventy years ago, Schlumberger invented a business called "wireline logging," a process by which a 10 foot long metal pole containing an electrical monitoring system was used to pinpoint the location of oil, gas, or water in a hole drilled for oil exploration.

Schlumberger carried this pole on a truck with a spool of wire connected to a data recording and analysis instrument. When a hole had been drilled, the pole was lowered to the bottom and was pulled up at 10 foot intervals. Every 10 feet, an electrical current was injected into the pole and a sensor on the pole recorded the electrical response of the surrounding geology. This response was fed back to the data recorder and, depending on the results of various tests, the Schlumberger field engineer could determine the depth at which the hydrocarbons were located.

Like HP, Schlumberger had a long tradition of engineers being the dominant function. In response to client demands for greater efficiency in their oil exploration processes, Schlumberger management decided to create a fundamental cultural change. This decision led to a new product development process that reduced cycle times by 50%. The most important element of this new process was the creation of product development teams. These teams consist of engineering and manufacturing specialists who share common managers and occupy new physical facilities designed specifically to accommodate these teams.

The relay race approach to product development that both these companies formerly used is well-established and continues today in many companies. In this process, R&D develops an innovation and tries to sell a business unit on turning the design into a revenue-generating product. If R&D succeeds in getting the business unit's attention, R&D may then supply the blueprints and an engineering model to the business unit manager.

The business unit may then supply these items to the sales and manufacturing departments. Frequently, the sales force responds that the innovation is not what customers want or it is two years too late (or too early) to generate significant revenues. Manufacturing may suggest that the innovation costs too much to make. It requires retooling the manufacturing line or purchasing supplies that are not available from an established supplier. After receiving this feedback, R&D may decide that the innovation is not worth pursuing, or it may take the feedback and redo its design. Although this relay race approach persists in many companies today, it slows time to market, raises development and product costs, and lowers market penetration as compared to the cross-functional team approach.

The cross-functional team approach strives to integrate functions. While the specific composition of these teams varies by industry and by company, it is typical for these teams to include specialists in disciplines such as engineering, manufacturing, finance, purchasing, logistics, marketing, customer service, and sales. Although these teams may be perceived as difficult to co-ordinate, they create fundamental benefits that far outweigh the cost of co-ordinating them.

» **Communication across functions lowers costs**. For example, in the "relay race" approach, if a design that R&D developed is too expensive to manufacture, a mutual blaming process consumes valuable time and resources. Cross-functional teams work more smoothly to achieve the shared objective of creating a product that offers competitively superior customer value.

» **Communication across functions reduces time**. At Schlumberger, for example, hand-offs between engineering and manufacturing have been reduced, leading to shorter product development cycles.

Technology leaders create financial and psychological incentives that reinforce cross-functional teams. As a result, team participants feel a sense of pride in what they are doing. Teams get a deeper understanding of how the skills of the entire organization can be co-ordinated to create superior value for customers.

DEPLOYING PROJECT PLANS

While project planning methods tend to vary by company and by industry, they share common objectives. Technology leaders want project plans to provide structure without constraining creativity. They use plans as a way of teaching new employees about the corporate culture, and they want project planning to create a common sense of direction for project development teams. Microsoft, Gillette and Merck offer interesting examples of how to structure projects.

Microsoft

Microsoft has a tradition of forging industry standards for desktop computing that create sustained high returns for shareholders. An essential component of its success is the way it plans its development projects. Microsoft uses activity-based planning that divides its projects into three broad phases: vision development, coding, and marketing. Its program managers develop a vision for the new product by melding their knowledge of customer needs with a deep understanding of the technology and where it is heading.

This vision is shared with developers. Developers are broken into many small teams that write the code. These development teams produce prototypes that are given to a select group of customers. These alpha and beta testers offer feedback regarding product features and usability.

Each night the various components of the system are joined together through a "build" process. "Bugs" found during the testing process are then fixed by the subteams that are responsible for these bugs. This process is repeated until most of the bugs are eliminated, or until management decides to ship the product, with the intention of distributing free "patches" at a later date. Finally, marketers introduce the new program at trade shows and develop and implement strategies to build revenues.

Gillette

The Gillette Company's Sensor Shaving System is one of the most successful new product introductions in history. It was introduced in 1990 and by 1995 was generating over $2.6bn in sales for Gillette. The initial prototype for the spring-mounted twin blade technology was developed in the early 1980s in a Gillette research lab in Britain. However, it took the threat of corporate takeover to galvanize the company into developing a new shaving system.

To develop the Sensor technology, Gillette scientists structured their research to gain insights into a variety of scientific fields. In particular, Gillette scientists studied the physiology of facial hair and skin. They researched the metallurgy of blade strength and sharpness. They analyzed the dynamics of a cartridge moving across skin. And they gained insight into the physics of a razor blade severing hair. The development project also focused on how these phenomena could interact to create a better shave.

Finally, by co-ordinating with manufacturing, R&D engineers developed a custom laser welder for making twin blade Sensor cartridges. The manufacturing/R&D team also created specialized scanning cameras for ensuring quality, enabling Gillette to become the lowest cost and highest quality manufacturer in the industry.

An improved version of the Sensor, the SensorExcel system, was launched in 1993. This system was initiated by an observation regarding the flow of skin during shaving. Gillette's technical team investigated ways of controlling this motion by various textured surfaces passing over the skin during shaving. This research led to the design of SensorExcel skin guard, a device composed of five raised, very fine microfins made of elastomer. Identical microfins were configured to form a precisely curving skin guard. These microfins stretched the skin, causing beard hairs to spring upwards so they could safely be cut more closely. They also increased the comfort of the shave by creating a pleasant tactile sensation on the face.

Furthermore, Gillette researchers improved the cartridge design to counterbalance the stretching effect required for closeness without producing a feeling of drag for the shaver. The solution that achieved this effect was a larger lubricating strip that increased lubrication and razor glide.

Merck

Merck organizes its product development projects into two broad phases: discovery and development. In the discovery phase, Merck allows scientists to use "rational drug design" techniques. Using these techniques, scientists experiment with the design of compounds with the potential to interrupt enzymes on the critical path of a major disease process such as arthritis, heart disease, cancer, and others. During this discovery phase, Merck may allow several small teams to experiment with possible solutions simultaneously.

Merck has developed "combinatorial libraries" that allow for rapid, automated synthesis and biological evaluation of millions of compounds. This process helps scientists to identify active families of compounds much more efficiently than a traditional "spray and pray" approach. Once an active compound is identified, technical specialists work together to design a compound that does the job safely. After formulations are developed, process chemists design an efficient and environmentally safe manufacturing process.

INVOLVING EARLY-ADOPTERS

Technology leaders involve early-adopters in the development of new products. Early-adopters are groups of customers that tend to be among the first to use a new technology. They tend to be highly creative and willing to work with technology developers to influence the ultimate design of a new product. Early-adopters often drive the purchase decisions of mass market "pragmatists", who seek the advice of the early-adopters regarding which vendor makes the best product in the category. Heartstream, Schlumberger and Intuit provide interesting examples of the economic benefits that emerge from involving early-adopters in the product development process.

Heartstream

Heartstream (acquired by HP in 1997) is a Seattle-based manufacturer of lightweight, easy-to-use, relatively inexpensive external defibrillators that can be used to revive an individual in the minutes following cardiac arrest. Heartstream worked closely with early-adopters in its target segment of cardiac arrest sufferers in public places such as stadiums, airports, casinos, cruise ships, and office buildings. Heartstream's research indicated that the survival rate after cardiac arrest is 90% if a victim is defibrillated after the first minute, declining by 7–10% after each incremental minute. Furthermore, Heartstream found that survival rates varied widely by city depending on how quickly the paramedics arrived at the scene of the cardiac arrest (1% survival rate in New York City, 25–30% in Seattle and as high as 50% in Rochester, Minnesota).

In working with early-adopters, Heartstream recognized that it could increase survival rates significantly. Heartstream developed a defibrillator that offered improvements over competing products in most of the features that customers cared about.

Specifically, Heartstream's ForeRunner weighs four pounds, requires minimal user training, demands no maintenance because it self-checks, requires its battery to be changed once a year, and costs about $3000.

Each of these attributes represented a significant improvement over traditional defibrillators. For example, traditional devices require extensive training and retraining every 90 days and demand battery testing up to three times a day. Furthermore, traditional devices weigh 15–20 pounds and cost up to $10,000.

Heartstream is targeting a multi-million dollar segment that it believes its larger competitors were late to understand and even later to respond to.

Schlumberger

Schlumberger developed its Logging While Drilling product to meet the specific needs of its early-adopters. Schlumberger listened to its offshore oil drilling customers, who conveyed a strong need for lowering the cost of oil exploration. This need was a result of 15 years of depressed oil prices, causing Schlumberger customers to slash their exploration budgets.

In its market survey, Schlumberger customers also expressed the need for accurate, timely, and high-quality tests. A cross-functional team of marketing and technical staff recognized that oil is typically found in thin, pancake-like formations that may be 10 feet high and miles wide. Schlumberger's offshore drilling clients typically drilled many vertical wells through these formations.

To meet this need, Schlumberger developed a much more efficient technology that enabled customers to drill only one well. This Logging While Drilling product performs the tests that customers need and corrects the direction of the drill as it penetrates horizontally through the oil in the formation. This product enabled British Petroleum, a Schlumberger client, to save $150mn that it had allocated to build an island off the southern coast of England. This island had been planned to enable BP to extract oil from a formation using the traditional vertical drilling technology.

Intuit

Intuit is unique in the software industry in its use of a consumer products business model. In developing Quicken, Intuit recognized that word-of-mouth was a more important driver of consumer software purchase decisions than salespeople, product advertisements or even magazine reviews. Intuit engineers often change software in direct response to user requests. They devote substantial energy to customer support and using customer feedback.

According to Bill Strauss, vice-president of operations, "We want our customers to be apostles for Intuit. Our goal is to make the customer feel so good about our products that they'll go out and tell six friends to buy them." Intuit's "Follow Me Home" program sends an Intuit employee home with a new Quicken user to watch the initial set-up process and take note of any confusion. Intuit subjects its products in development to beta tests and intensive scrutiny from a full range of users from novices to experts.

In October 1993, Intuit introduced its Usability Research Lab, a facility dedicated to enhancing the interaction between Intuit and its customer. At this center, focus groups and customer advisory panels provide input to the software development process from the prototype stage throughout the life of the product. Finally, hundreds of customer comment cards and letters are scrutinized by Intuit's Marketing and Development teams, resulting in information that is applied to the creation of each new product.

Involving early-adopters in the product development process is a simple yet radical notion for many technology companies. The technique is radical because it suggests that not all good product ideas spring from the minds of scientists and engineers. In order for the technique to be effective, the input of early-adopters must be accepted and understood by the new product design team.

CEO CHANGE AGENDA

A company's ability to capture the benefits of a winning product development process depends on two factors. First, a company should compare its product development process with that used by technology leaders. Second, the company should assess the CEO's willingness to lead change. If there are significant opportunities for improvement and the CEO is willing to lead the change process, the following strategic initiatives are suggested.

» **Pick a prototype organization**. HP decided to test the new product development process in its Vancouver division. This division needed to succeed with its printer product as a condition of its continued survival. As a result, the development team had a powerful incentive to change in a way that would create value for customers. At the same time, all project participants recognized that they had the support and attention of senior management. The result was a new process that involved close co-operation between engineering, manufacturing and marketing, leading to a substantial new business.

» **Competitive analysis**. HP was able to make a fundamental change in its product development process after it had identified a competitor that it truly respected. By studying Canon, a world leader in laser printer technology, HP created a focus for its change effort. In general, a fundamental change should begin by looking at the company strategically – examining in an objective way how the company is positioned in its industry relative to its customers, competitors and technology.

» **Reward success**. Since the organization will be watching closely to see how management treats the participants in the prototype organization, it is critical that they be rewarded visibly. In addition, the success of the team should be incorporated into the company's success "mythology."

» **Let the change grow organically**. After witnessing the success of HP's Vancouver division, other operating units began to emulate its practices. As these practices are adopted by other operating units, however, it is important to reinforce their adoption by changing performance evaluation and incentive systems to reinforce the new process.

Key Concepts and Thinkers

There are many thinkers and concepts that form the foundation of the management of technological innovation. The lexicon of innovation management concepts in this chapter covers:

» key concepts; and
» key thinkers.

Activity Based Planning - Cusumano and Selby describe a Microsoft process for product design called Activity Based Planning (ABP). ABP bases product feature selection and prioritization on user activities and data. Prior to its adoption of ABP, Microsoft often chose product features based on who shouted loudest in a product development meeting. As a result, features that were included often did not meet customer needs, while features that customers wanted were often excluded. To solve these problems, Microsoft developed ABP.

ABP begins with a systematic study of user activities for actions such as writing letters or doing a budget. Microsoft then evaluates product features in terms of how well they support important or frequent user activities. The benefits are more rational discussions of feature trade-offs, better rankings of what customers want to do, more focused debates on whether a particular feature facilitates a particular task, more readable specifications, and better synchronization among marketing, user education, and product development.

Big Hairy Audacious Goals (BHAGs) - Collins and Porras note that BHAGs differ from traditional goals in that BHAGs commit organizations to a huge daunting challenge that is clear and compelling and serves as a unifying focal point of effort. BHAGs have a clear finish line so the organization can know when it has achieved the goal. An example of a BHAG is US President Kennedy's proclamation in May 1961 that the US should "commit itself to achieving the goal, before this decade is out, of landing a man on the moon and returning him safely to earth." Although scientists gave this BHAG a 50% chance of success, Congress committed $549mn to the goal immediately and billions thereafter.

Bundling - Cusumano and Selby describe a Microsoft process for product design called bundling. Bundling implies that Microsoft combines functions that had previously been performed in separate products. Microsoft believes that bundling makes its products more useful to customers at a lower price, thereby enabling Microsoft to increase the size of its market by billions of new customers who are attracted to the irresistible value proposition of being able to do more and more with their computers at a lower and lower price. A byproduct of the bundling strategy is that Microsoft's competitors are often unable to keep up with Microsoft's bundling strategy.

Simply put, by lowering the price at which customers can obtain its products, Microsoft harms those competitors who are unable to earn a profit at such low price levels.

Chasm, The - The gap in purchasing a new technology between the early-adopters and the pragmatists. If a firm cannot cross the chasm, e.g. encourage the pragmatists to purchase the product that the early-adopters have tried, then the firm usually goes under. In order to cross the chasm, Moore advises firms to develop a high payoff application of their technology for a specific industry sector, such as financial services or drug discovery. If a specific industry sector achieves significant economic benefits, then it is likely that pragmatists from other industries will buy the product.

Christensen, Clayton – Clayton M. Christensen is a professor of business administration at the Harvard Business School. His research and writing interests center on the management of technological innovation, developing organizational capabilities, and finding new markets for new technologies.

Dr Christensen's book, *The Innovator's Dilemma: When New Technologies Cause Great Firms to Fail*, won the 1997 Global Business Book Award. *The Innovator's Dilemma* was based on, in Christensen's own words: "what can cause smart people to make wrong decisions." The lessons he learned from his extensive research provide a framework for detecting and countering disruptive technologies. Among his consulting clients are Intel, Hewlett-Packard, Compaq, Lucent, and Eastman Kodak.

Prior to joining the Harvard Business School faculty, Dr Christensen served as chairman and president of Ceramics Process Systems Corporation, a firm he co-founded with several MIT professors. Dr Christensen was also a White House Fellow and former assistant to US Transportation Secretaries Drew Lewis and Elizabeth Dole. He holds a BA in economics from Brigham Young University; an M.Phil. in economics from Oxford University, where he studied as a Rhodes Scholar; and an MBA and DBA from the Harvard Business School.

Clock Building, Not Time Telling – In defining the characteristics of companies that are likely to survive long-term, Collins and Porras distinguish between Time Telling, e.g. having a great business idea of a charismatic leader, and Clock Building, e.g. building a company that can prosper beyond the presence of a single leader and through multiple product life cycles.

Collins, Jim – Jim Collins operates a management education and consulting practice in Palo Alto, CA. He is the co-author of *Beyond Entrepreneurship*[1] and a recipient of the Distinguished Teaching Award at Stanford University Graduate School of Business, whose faculty he joined in 1988. Previously he held positions at McKinsey & Company and Hewlett-Packard.

Cult-like cultures – Collins and Porras suggest that companies that survive long-term have very strong cultures that inspire intense devotion to the company, much of which is related to the characteristics of the individuals who best exemplify the beliefs of the company. A corollary of these cult-like cultures is that companies eject individuals who do not fit with the culture very quickly, just as the human immune system ejects viruses.

Cusumano, Michael – Michael A. Cusumano is the Sloan Management Review Distinguished Professor at the Massachusetts Institute of Technology's Sloan School of Management. He specializes in strategy and technology management in the computer software, automobile, and consumer electronics industries. He teaches courses on Strategic Management as well as The Software Business, and works extensively as a consultant in software development, strategic planning, and technology strategy, primarily for high-tech companies.

Professor Cusumano received a BA degree from Princeton University in 1976 and a PhD from Harvard University in 1984. He completed a postdoctoral fellowship in the Production and Operations Management Area at the Harvard Business School during 1984–6. He is fluent in Japanese and has lived and worked in Japan for seven years. While in Japan, he held two Fulbright Fellowships and a Japan Foundation Fellowship for studying at Tokyo University. He has been a visiting professor in management at Hitotsubashi University and Tokyo University in Japan, and the University of St Gallen in Switzerland, and a visiting professor in computer science at the University of Maryland. Professor Cusumano has consulted for major companies around the world. He is on the advisory board of the MIT Internet & Telecommunications Convergence Consortium and is chairman of the board of the MIT Sloan Management Review. He also writes periodically for *The Wall Street Journal*, *Computerworld*, *The Washington Post*, and other business publications.

Professor Cusumano is the author or co-author of five books. His latest book, *Competing on Internet Time: Lessons from Netscape and its Battle with Microsoft*[2] examines the competition between Netscape and Microsoft, as well as techniques for managing strategic planning and software development in fast-paced, unpredictable markets. This was named one of the top 10 business books of 1998 by *Business Week* and Amazon, and played a central role in the Microsoft antitrust trial.

Microsoft Secrets is an international best-seller, with approximately 150,000 copies in print in 14 languages. This book explores the principles behind Microsoft's competitive strategy, organization, management systems, and processes for software development, testing, and project management.

Thinking Beyond Lean: How Multi-Project Management is Transforming Product Development at Toyota and Other Companies[3] analyzes product development strategies and organizational structures in the auto industry that center around sharing platforms and other key components in multiple projects managed concurrently.

He has also written *Japan's Software Factories: A Challenge to US Management*[4] and *The Japanese Automobile Industry: Technology and Management at Nissan and Toyota*,[5] and some 70 articles or papers on software engineering management, high-tech entrepreneurship, consumer electronics development, manufacturing process innovation, and management of product development teams. He is currently finishing a book about platform leadership and complementary innovation in high-tech industries with Annabelle Gawer of INSEAD.

Disruptive technology – Christensen defines a disruptive technology as a new product or service that isn't as good as the firm's current product line; therefore, it doesn't appeal to the firm's best customers. Typically, the disruptive technology is technologically simple. Often, it's more convenient to use. But it's less expensive, and the firm make slower gross margin dollars per unit sold. So it's not a discontinuous improvement in technology. It's something that's cheaper, simpler, and often smaller. For example, at Digital Equipment, personal computers really weren't important to Digital's bottom line until the game was over. And as soon as the personal computer makers could start to pick off Digital's customers, they were in fact bigger than Digital.

Early-adopters – Are a group of customers that Moore defines as those that want to be the first to try a new technology. Early-adopters typically try a technology and have a group of less adventurous business acquaintances who wait to see whether the technology is working well for the early-adopter before purchasing the technology themselves.

Foster, Richard – Richard Foster is a director of McKinsey & Company, Inc., New York City, NY. He was a winner of the IRI's 1986 Maurice Holland Award. Foster joined McKinsey in 1973 and has become widely known for his work on improving the innovative performance of large organizations. He recently led McKinsey's global knowledge-building activities. The author of *Innovation: The Attacker's Advantage*,[6] Foster is currently working on a second book, tentatively titled *The Practical Arts of Creative Destruction*. He holds a doctorate in engineering and applied science from Yale University.

In *Innovation*, Foster offers several examples of the S-curve and limits with regards to innovation and technology and technological change. He considers innovation as a repeatable economic event and examines using the S-curve as a forecasting tool. The book looks at leaders and losers in several US industries. The Appendix asks key questions to determine management processes and systems ability to detect discontinuities.

Genius of the "AND" versus tyranny of the "OR" – In defining the pragmatic idealism of companies that are likely to survive long-term, Collins and Porras distinguish between the genius of the "AND," e.g., companies that are able to make decisions that provide both long-term business benefits and good short-term public perceptions of the company and the tyranny of the "OR," e.g., the need to make an explicit choice between long-term business benefits and short-term profits – with the typical emphasis being placed on short-term profits.

Innovator's Dilemma, The – Christensen notes that it makes sense for an organization to focus single-mindedly on its best customers, and to give them the products that improve the organization's competitiveness in the most profitable regions of its product line. The organization should just keep weeding out the products where it doesn't make money – that's the right thing to do. If organizations don't do that, they're going to lose fast to their competition. But the dilemma occurs when disruptive technologies come into their market at the bottom: then organizations have got to invest in what doesn't make sense for them. The dilemma is that if they don't focus all their energy on upgrading their product line, and focus on being more and more competitive through existing customers, they'll fail. But if they don't focus on the disruptive technology, they'll fail as well. And Christensen notes that it is impossible to do both. The solution, according to Christensen, is to set up a different company that has a different focus – and then let it go after the disruptive technology. Let the mainstream company keep doing what it's doing well – it's got to do that in order to survive, and you don't want it to lose that focus.

Intellect management – Quinn's concept is that increasingly the power of a modern corporation lies more in its intellectual and service capabilities than in its hard assets such as land, plant and equipment. Quinn argues that as a result, the ability to manage people in order to enhance the value of a firm's intellectual assets (e.g. technological know-how, product design, marketing presentation, understanding of customers, and innovation) is of increasing importance. As a result, Quinn suggests that firms must find ways to harness and build the value of their intellectual assets in order to increase shareholder value.

Moore, Geoffrey – Geoffrey Moore is a managing director with The Chasm Group, a consulting practice based in California that provides market development and business strategy services to many leading high-technology companies. He is also a venture partner with Mohr Davidow Ventures, a California-based venture capital firm specializing in specific technology markets, including e-commerce, Internet, enterprise software, networking and semiconductors. As a venture partner at Mohr Davidow, he provides market strategy advice to their high-tech portfolio companies. Moore is a frequent speaker and lecturer at industry conferences and his books are required reading at Stanford, Harvard, MIT, and other leading business schools.

Moore's current practice focuses on the concepts of his recent book *Living on the Fault Line*, targeted at CEOs and senior executives of Fortune 500 companies facing the impact of the Internet.

Moore's first book, *Crossing the Chasm*, initially published in 1991, adds compelling new extensions to the classical model of the Technology Adoption Life Cycle. He introduces his readers to a gap or "chasm" that innovative companies and their products must cross in order to reach the lucrative mainstream market. A revised edition was released in July 1999 to update industries and case-study companies.

The sequel, *Inside the Tornado*, published in 1995, provides readers with insight into how to capitalize on the potential for hypergrowth beyond the chasm. This second book sorts out how the market forces behind the Technology Adoption Life Cycle demand the need for radical shifts in market strategy.

The Gorilla Game, Moore's third book, was originally published in March of 1998, with a revised version, including a new chapter on internet investing, released August 2000. This book was co-authored with Chasm Group managing partner and high-tech marketing strategist Tom Kippola, and stock investment guru and BancAmerica Robertson Stephens analyst Paul Johnson. *The Gorilla Game* combines the methodology Moore introduced in *Crossing the Chasm* and *Inside the Tornado* with Johnson's stock market valuation models and Wall Street expertise, and Kippola's high-tech investment experience.

Moore's newest book, *Living on the Fault Line*, focuses on a single theme: how should the management of a public company that rose to prominence prior to the age of the Internet manage for shareholder value now that the Internet is upon us? *Living on the Fault Line* guides executives and managers who are coping with disruptive technology destabilizing their core market positions, providing them with new models, metrics, and organizational practices to meet the challenges of the new economy.

Prior to founding The Chasm Group in 1992, Moore was a principal and partner at Regis McKenna, Inc., a leading high-tech marketing strategy and marketing communications company. For the decade prior to this, he was a sales and marketing executive at three different software companies.

Moore holds a bachelor's degree from Stanford University and a PhD from the University of Washington, both in literature, and served as an English professor at Olivet College.

Outsourcing – Quinn's concept that a company should identify those value chain activities in which it is a world-class performer and contract out the performance of activities in the field of which the firm is not a leader. Quinn's concept, while fine in theory, brings with it important practical challenges. For example, if a firm outsources an activity to a third party, the firm needs a way to measure and incentivize the firm to whom the activity is being outsourced, to ensure that the outsourced activity is consistently being performed at a world-class level of performance. Too frequently, firms have undertaken outsourcing assignments only to discover that they are not able to perform the activities as well as they had promised. A consequence is that many firms ended up insourcing the activities that they had previously outsourced.

Porras, Jerry – Jerry Porras is the Fred H. Merrill Professor of Organizational Behavior and Change at Stanford University Graduate School of Business. He is the author of *Stream Analysis*[7] and the co-inventor of stream analysis computer software used for organizational change diagnosis. He also directs Stanford's Executive Program in Organizational Change. Previously he held positions at General Electric and Lockheed.

Pragmatists – A group of customers that Moore defines as those that will only purchase a new technology when its costs and benefits have become clear. Pragmatists typically will wait until the early-adopters are achieving great success with the new technology. Since pragmatists represent the biggest portion of the market, it is crucial for the long-term success of a high-tech product that the pragmatists ultimately end up buying.

Preserve the core and stimulate progress – In developing an important manifestation of the concept of the Genius of the "AND," Collins and Porras highlight companies that are able to both preserve the core, e.g. companies with a core ideology that provides continuity and stability and companies that stimulate progress by urging continual change and movement.

Product Improvement Initiatives – Cusumano and Selby describe how Microsoft established a Product Improvement Group in 1991 to provide customer feedback for product developers. This customer feedback is processed into a prioritized list of Product Improvement Initiatives. These initiatives are based on information from a variety of sources including customer service calls, the observations from Microsoft's user research and usability testing, and product usage studies. The basic concept of Product Improvement Initiatives is that user feedback generates ideas for increasing the value of Microsoft's products and improving Microsoft's competitiveness.

Quinn, James Brian – James Brian Quinn is professor emeritus at Dartmouth's Amos Tuck School of Management. Quinn taught Tuck's TYCOON Business Simulation, Entrepreneurship, and Technology and Management courses. A member of the faculty from 1957–93, he is William and Josephine Buchanan Professor of Management Emeritus and continues to teach in executive education programs worldwide.

His recent books, *Intelligent Enterprise*[8] and *Innovation Explosion*,[9] were seminal works in developing the strategies and organizations that have led to the $350bn outsourcing industry. They provide a model for how business and innovation will be conducted in the twenty-first century, changing the way people work worldwide and how economists think about growth in both developed and developing countries.

Selby, Richard – Richard W. Selby is an Associate Professor of Information and Computer Science at the University of California, Irvine. He received his PhD in computer science from the University of Maryland in 1985. He has published over 60 technical and management articles on software engineering, focusing on software quality and process improvement, software measurement and analysis, and software tools and environments. He has received over $9mn in research funding from DARPA, National Science Foundation, and industrial sponsors including IBM, TRW, Hughes, and NASA. He has consulted worldwide for numerous commercial, defense, aerospace, telecommunications, and government organizations. He founded Amadeus Software Research, Inc., which develops and distributes a market-leading software measurement tool. He has held visiting faculty positions at the Massachusetts Institute of Technology and Osaka University, Japan. He is the co-author of the book *Microsoft Secrets* which was ranked as the number 6 best-selling hardcover business book by *Business Week*.[10]

Synch and Stabilize Process – Cusumano and Selby describe how Microsoft structures its product development process to make a large organization function as a collection of smaller, more productive sub-groups. Cusumano and Selby term this product development process "Synch and Stabilize." Synch and Stabilize is an approach to product development that continuously synchronizes what people are doing as individuals and members of different teams, and periodically stabilizes the product as the project proceeds rather than once at the end. The basic purpose of the Synch and Stabilize approach is to make software development more productive. The idea is that since user needs for software are often difficult to specify beforehand, it is better to build prototypes and gather customer feedback while at the same time co-ordinating the efforts of different development functions such as design, building, and testing.

Sustaining technologies – Christensen defines sustaining technologies as those that improve the value of an existing product for an existing customer.

Try a lot of stuff and keep what works – Collins and Porras suggest that long-term survivors find some of their best new products and services not through detailed strategic planning but through opportunistic experimentation. Collins and Porras use the notion "try a lot of stuff and keep what works" to define this approach. For example, in 1890, Johnson & Johnson, then a supplier of antiseptic gauze and medical plasters, received a letter from a physician complaining about patient skin irritation from certain plasters. Johnson & Johnson's director of research responded by sending Italian talc to apply to the skin. He then convinced Johnson & Johnson to send a can of talc as part of the standard package with certain products. Soon customers began asking for the talc alone – leading to the creation of "Johnson's Toilet and Baby Powder," a very famous product used around the world.

Utterback, James – James M. Utterback is Professor of Management and Engineering; Chair of The MIT Management of Technology

Program. Utterback, who looks at the emergence of dominant product designs, studies how to develop products in keeping with a company's overall strategy. He also considers how to move concepts effectively to market. In his book *Mastering the Dynamics of Innovation*,[11] he focuses on the creative and destructive effects of technological change on the life of a company.

von Hippel, Eric – Eric von Hippel is a Professor at the MIT Sloan School of Management, specializing in Innovation Management. von Hippel discovers and explores patterns in the sources of innovation. For example, von Hippel finds that, contrary to conventional wisdom, successful innovations are often first developed and tested by product or service users themselves – "lead users" – rather than by the firms that are first to bring those innovations to market.

Von Hippel's research and consulting is directed towards two major goals:

» improving understanding of how the innovation process works; and
» developing new innovation processes for industry that can identify "breakthrough" innovations more systematically and quickly.

NOTES

1 Collins, J. (1992) *Beyond Entrepreneurship – Turning Your Business Into an Enduring Great Company*. Prentice-Hall, Englewood Cliffs, NJ.

2 Cusumano, M. and Yoffie, D. (1998) *Competing on Internet Time: Lessons from Netscape and its Battle with Microsoft*. The Free Press, New York, NY.

3 Cusumano, M. and Nobeoka, K. (1998) *Thinking Beyond Lean: How Multi-Project Management is Transforming Product Development at Toyota and Other Companies*. The Free Press, New York, NY.

4 Cusumano, M. (1991) *Japan's Software Factories: A Challenge to US Management*. Oxford University Press, New York, NY.

5 Cusumano, M. (1985) *The Japanese Automobile Industry: Technology and Management at Nissan and Toyota*. Harvard University Press, Cambridge, MA.

6 Foster, R. (1986) *Innovation: The Attacker's Advantage*. Summit Books, New York, NY.

7 Porras, J. (1987) *Stream Analysis*. Addison-Wesley Publishing, Reading, MA.

8 Quinn, J. (1992) *Intelligent Enterprise*. The Free Press, New York, NY.

9 Quinn, J., Baruch, J., and Zien, K. (1997) *Innovation Explosion*. The Free Press, New York, NY.

10 *Business Week*, November 27, 1995.

11 Utterback, J. (1994) *Mastering the Dynamics of Innovation*. Harvard Business School Press, Boston, MA.

Resources

There are many useful resources on the management of innovation. This chapter identifies the best such resources, including:

» books;
» articles; and
» selected Web sites.

Alster, N. (1995) "Making the kids stand on their own." *Forbes*, October 9.

Cauley, L. (1996) "Bell Atlantic, Nynex, PacTel to Close Tele-TV." *Wall Street Journal*, December 6, A3, A10.

Clark, D. (1996) "A Dud At Its Birth, Windows NT Is Back As A Networking Force." *Wall Street Journal*, July 29, A1, A4.

Cohan, P. (1997) *The Technology Leaders: How America's Most Profitable High-Tech Companies Innovate Their Way to Success*. Jossey-Bass, San Francisco, CA.

Management consultant Peter S. Cohan's *The Technology Leaders* presents a revealing look at the way 20 of today's top high-tech companies are building profits through ingenuity and invention. The unifying thread among winning firms in such rapidly changing fields as biotechnology, computer hardware, and environmental services, Cohan argues, is their ability to consistently introduce visionary new products that grab market share, generate additional capital, and then allow the cycle to start anew. After showing how companies like Amgen, US Robotics and Thermo Electron are doing it, he offers an "Innovation Scorecard" for self-assessment and developing a plan for change.

Collins, J. and Porras, J. (1994) *Built To Last: Successful Habits of Visionary Companies*. HarperBusiness, New York, NY.

This analysis of what makes great companies great has been hailed everywhere as an instant classic and one of the best business titles since *In Search of Excellence*. The authors, James C. Collins and Jerry I. Porras, spent six years in research, and they freely admit that their own preconceptions about business success were devastated by their actual findings – along with the preconceptions of virtually everyone else.

Built to Last identifies 18 "visionary" companies and sets out to determine what's special about them. To get on the list, a company had to be world famous, have a stellar brand image, and be at least 50 years old. We're talking about companies that even a layperson knows to be, well, different: the Disneys, the Wal-Marts, the Mercks.

Whatever the key to the success of these companies, the key to the success of this book is that the authors don't waste time comparing them to business failures. Instead, they use a control group of "successful-but-second-rank" companies to highlight what's special about their 18 "visionary" picks. Thus Disney is compared to Columbia Pictures, Ford to GM, Hewlett-Packard to Texas Instruments, and so on.

The core myth, according to the authors, is that visionary companies must start with a great product and be pushed into the future by charismatic leaders. There are examples of that pattern, they admit: Johnson & Johnson, for one. But there are also just too many counterexamples – in fact, the majority of the "visionary" companies, including giants like 3M, Sony, and TI, don't fit the model. They were characterized by total lack of an initial business plan or key idea and by remarkably self-effacing leaders. Collins and Porras are much more impressed with something else they shared: an almost cult-like devotion to a "core ideology" or identity, and active indoctrination of employees into "ideological commitment" to the company.

The comparison with the business "B"-team does tend to raise a significant methodological problem: which companies are to be counted as "visionary" in the first place? There's an air of circularity here, as if you achieve "visionary" status by ... achieving visionary status. So many roads lead to Rome that the book is less practical than it might appear. But that's exactly the point of an eloquent chapter on 3M. This wildly successful company had no master plan, little structure, and no prima donnas. Instead it had an atmosphere in which bright people were both keen to see the company succeed and unafraid to "try a lot of stuff and keep what works."

Cusumano, M. and Selby, R. (1995) *Microsoft Secrets: How the World's Most Powerful Software Company Creates Technology, Shapes Markets, and Manages People*. The Free Press, New York, NY.

A factual examination of how Microsoft works, both internally, and in the market place. Unlike the raft of gossipy Bill-bios or sardonic and shrill pro- or anti- screeds, this book is focused clearly (if sometimes ploddingly) on one central question: the relationship between business strategies and software development.

Dolan, K. (1996) "Help Wanted: Urgent!" *Forbes*, October 7, p. 18.
"EMC Is The One To Beat." *Information Week*, May 1, 1995.

HP Labs: http://www.hpl.hp.com/about/overview.htm.

Ingrassia, L. (1992) "The Cutting Edge." *Wall Street Journal*, April 6.

Kaplan, J. (1994) *Startup: A Silicon Valley Adventure*. Penguin Books, New York, NY.

The founder of the visionary, yet doomed, GO Corporation kept notes throughout his years at the helm, thinking that one day he would produce a book. It shows. This is a vivid and lively rise-and-fall account of a company born to create a pen-based computer. It begins on a corporate jet with the author and fellow industry visionary Mitchell Kapor, founder of Lotus, sharing a vision of pen computing. From there, Startup quickly leaps to the day-to-day challenges of hiring staff, constantly reassessing and readjusting goals, and coping with the stress of endless rounds of venture capital funding. That Kaplan, in his first attempt at running a company, battles with the top forces at Microsoft, IBM, and other industry giants to bring the idea to market, only makes the story more compelling. His company's ultimate failure says more about a cutthroat industry than about the quality of Kaplan's product.

Klaus, T. (1993) "Checking Out Linux." *Unixworld*, March 1993.

Levine, J. (1996) "'A' is for arbitrage." *Forbes*, July 15.

Loeb, M. (1995) "Ten Commandments for Managing Creative People." *Fortune*, January 16.

Markoff, J. (1995) "Microsoft Quietly Puts Together Computer Research Laboratory." *The New York Times*, December 11.

Moore, G. (1995) *Inside The Tornado*. HarperBusiness, New York, NY.

Explains the market dynamics behind high-tech hypergrowth. *Inside the Tornado*, the sequel to *Crossing the Chasm* by Silicon Valley marketing strategist Geoffrey Moore, is required reading material for business schools and industry pundits. The book focuses on the market dynamics of hypergrowth, with a look at how companies such as Microsoft and Netscape capture dominant market shares and leap into prominence.

Moore's first book, *Crossing the Chasm*, introduced readers to an updated view of the Technology Adoption Life Cycle, including a "chasm" phase which separates the early-adopters from the mainstream market of pragmatic customers, and the strategies for making this market transition.

Inside the Tornado extends Moore's work with the Technology Adoption Life Cycle model to incorporate three distinct mainstream market stages – a pre-hypergrowth era of niche markets, the mass-market phenomenon of hypergrowth itself, and a post-hypergrowth era of mass customization. Moore illustrates the dynamics of each stage with examples from cutting-edge companies such as Hewlett-Packard, Microsoft, Intel, Sybase, PeopleSoft and Lotus. He then goes on to analyze each stage's impact on strategic partnerships, competitive advantage, positioning, and organizational leadership.

Moore says, "The biggest challenge for management is that with each market phase transition, a new business strategy is called for – one that is not only different from their current strategy, but actually contradicts some of its core principles."

Inside the Tornado reaches out to companies beyond high-tech who are in technology-enabled or leveraged businesses, where the same market dynamics apply: publishing and broadcasting, banking and finance, healthcare, as well as entertainment, and retail, where market forces are driving rapid innovation and new leaders are appearing overnight.

The critical success factor in each of these competitions, according to Moore, is to achieve "gorilla status" inside the tornado in order to be the market leader during the hypergrowth phase, which results in permanent advantages throughout the remainder of the life cycle. Timing is critical to this tornado strategy. Moore explains how to pool resources and gain supporters during the pre-tornado phase and then how to unleash them once the tornado hits.

He also helps companies understand the post-tornado transition to a maturing market when companies must refocus on winning additional business from their installed base instead of seeking revenue growth from new customers.

Nee, E. (1996) "Interview with John Chambers." *Upside*, July.

Peltz, M. (1996) "High tech's premier venture capitalist." *Institutional Investor*, June.

Porter, M. (1980) *Competitive Strategy: Techniques for Analyzing Industries and Competitors*. The Free Press, New York, NY.

Michael E. Porter's *Competitive Strategy* analyses industries, capturing the complexity of industry competition in five underlying forces. Porter introduces three generic strategies – lowest cost, differentiation, and focus – which bring structure to the task of strategic positioning. He shows how competitive advantage can be defined in terms of relative cost and relative prices, thus linking it directly to profitability, and presents a perspective on how profit is created and divided.

Porter, M. (1985) *Competitive Advantage: Creating and Sustaining Superior Performance.* The Free Press, New York, NY.

The complement to *Competitive Strategy*, Michael E. Porter's *Competitive Advantage* explores the underpinnings of competitive advantage in the individual firm. With 30 printings in English and translated into 13 languages, this volume describes how a firm actually gains an advantage over its rivals. *Competitive Advantage* introduces a whole new way of understanding what a firm does. Porter's concept of the value chain disaggregates a company into "activities," or the discrete functions or processes that represent the elemental building blocks of competitive advantage.

Competitive Advantage takes strategy from broad vision to an internally consistent configuration of activities. Its framework provides the tools to understand the drivers of cost and a company's relative cost position. Porter's value chain enables managers to isolate the underlying sources of buyer value that will command a premium price, and the reasons why one product or service substitutes for another. He shows how competitive advantage lies not only in activities themselves but in the way activities relate to each other, to supplier activities, and to customer activities. *Competitive Advantage* also provides for the first time the tools to strategically segment an industry and rigorously assess the competitive logic of diversification.

"Quotes on David Packard." *San Jose Mercury News*, March 27, 1996.
Steadman, C. (1995) "IBM drops RAID boost; costs, complexity may rise." *ComputerWorld*, February 20.
Stephens, M. "Revenge of the Nerds." [PBS television broadcast], October 1996.

Stross, R. (1996) *The Microsoft Way: The Real Story of How the Company Outsmarts Its Competition.* Addison-Wesley, Reading, MA.

An overview of Microsoft, the enterprise that dominates the widening world of PC programming. Granted open access to Microsoft's files and staff, Stross eschewed a traditional corporate history in favor of a four-part audit that puts Microsoft and Bill Gates (its co-founder) in a clearer perspective than that found in the eyes of rivals or antitrust lawyers. The author (Business/San Jose State Univ.) first examines Microsoft's personnel policies and operational practices; he concludes that hiring smart people for financially rewarding as well as professionally challenging assignments, and a willingness to commit sizable sums to R&D, rank among the principal secrets of Microsoft's continuing success. Stross goes on to review how Microsoft conducted a campaign to break into consumer outlets (most notably, with a CD-ROM encyclopedia dubbed Encarta), and the stiff competition it faces from Intuit in personal finance software. Covered as well are Microsoft's efforts to develop a commercial stake in interactive TV, its late start in the Internet market, and the attention of Justice Department attorneys. Stross finishes with a chapter on the philanthropic purposes to which a Gates might put his billions.

Tanouye, E. (1996) "Value of Some Drug Firms' Acquisitions Is Questioned." *Wall Street Journal*, November 18.
Trachtenberg, J. (1996) "How Philips Flubbed Its US Introduction of Electronic Product." *Wall Street Journal*, June 28, pages A1 and A4.
Utterback, J. (1996) *Mastering the Dynamics of Innovation.* Harvard Business School Press, Boston, MA.

Utterback describes the underlying nature of what drives new innovation, where it comes from, where to look for it and how to adapt.

He recognizes that a sole focus on customers' needs can lead a company and its products to extinction. Sometimes the customer does not want new and improved. Sometimes they want different and better.

Utterback explains that companies that gain dominance in their industries tend to hold on to it by reducing their costs and increasing their competence in what they do. This makes it hard for new entry by upstarts using the same path. What is clear after reading, is that upstarts don't always use the same path and can attack at unexpected angles.

Utterback provides clear example after example of companies that were totally unwilling to focus any energy towards emerging technologies and then were swept away by a wave of innovative technology that left them and their stockholders caught in the undertow.

von Hippel, E. (1988) *The Sources of Innovation*. Oxford University Press, New York, NY.

It has long been assumed that new product innovations are typically developed by product manufacturers, an assumption that has inevitably had a major impact on innovation-related research and activities ranging from how firms organize their research and development to how governments measure innovation. In this synthesis of his seminal research, von Hippel challenges that basic assumption and demonstrates that innovation occurs in different places in different industries.

Presenting a series of studies showing that end-users, material suppliers, and others are the typical sources of innovation in some fields, von Hippel explores why this variation in the "functional" sources of innovation occurs and how it might be predicted. He also proposes and tests some implications of replacing a manufacturer-as-innovator assumption with a view of the innovation process as predictably distributed across users, manufacturers, and suppliers. Innovation, he argues, will take place where there is greatest economic benefit to the innovator.

Wilke, J. (1996) "Thermo Electron Uses An Unusual Strategy To Create Products." *Wall Street Journal*, August 5.
Yoder, S. (1994) "How H-P Used Tactics Of the Japanese to Beat Them at Their Game." *Wall Street Journal*, September 8.

Eight Steps to Technology Leadership

Putting the management secrets of the technology leaders into practice is easier said than done. This final chapter helps managers adapt their organizations to achieve the performance-enhancing characteristics of technology leaders by covering the following steps:

» use the "Innovation Scorecard" as a diagnostic tool;
» pick a "trial" division;
» build a "change team;"
» develop a change plan;
» map the current process;
» study the process of "admired" companies;
» design a new process; and
» train the rest of the organization.

How can we be more innovative?

This is the key question in the minds of CEOs in technology companies around the world.

Here we present a framework that companies can use to help answer this question. It is predicated on two key assumptions: first, that innovation produces measurable economic value; and, second, that companies can identify and improve the way they manage the business processes that drive "return on innovation."

This "Innovation Scorecard" framework provides the basis for evaluating improving the innovativeness of a firm, and hence its return on innovation.

RETURN ON INNOVATION

Companies use a variety of ways to measure the concept of return on innovation. In general, the greater the degree of analytical precision in the calculation, the less widespread will be the use of the measure. The advantages and disadvantages of various measures are described below.

Percent of current year sales from new products

As mentioned earlier, many companies use this measure to assess how well they are doing at innovation. This measure has the advantage of being fairly easy for companies to calculate if they track revenues by product. On the other hand, if a company generates 30% of its current year sales from products introduced in the last five years, how is the company to determine whether that performance is good relative to competitors? Furthermore, if a company takes a year to develop and market a technology that it had licensed from a university researcher and if this technology led to a $100mn product, its value to the company would probably be much greater than if a product with the same revenue stream had taken 10 years to develop internally and had been introduced to the market 18 months later.

Return on equity

This measure has the obvious disadvantage of being a very crude gauge of the value of investments in innovation. Shareholder's equity is allocated for activities other than innovation. On the other hand, return on equity, particularly averaged over a five year period, is a good measure of a company's overall performance relative to its industry. Furthermore, comparable statistics are available for publicly traded companies. In addition, to the extent that the company has estimated its cost of capital, the relationship between return on equity and cost of capital could be a useful approximation of return on innovation.

Profits per employee

Like return on equity, this measure has the obvious disadvantage of being a very crude gauge of returns from innovation. Relative profits per employee may well be driven by other factors besides innovation. On the other hand, profits per employee is a good measure of a company's productivity relative to its industry, and comparable statistics are available for publicly traded companies.

Stock price increase

To a greater extent than return on equity, this measure has the obvious disadvantage of being driven by factors other than the returns from innovation. Changes in stock price over, say, a five year period are probably driven by many factors. These factors include changes in interest rates and quarterly earnings performance relative to expectations. On the other hand, percentage change in stock price of technology leaders tended to exceed that of peer companies over the period of time analyzed. Furthermore, comparative statistics are widely available.

Return on innovation

The concept of return on innovation should be measured by calculating the net present value of the cash flows associated with specific product and process innovations. While this measure has the advantage of providing management with an accurate accounting of the value that investments in innovation generate for the company, it has several short-term disadvantages. In particular, since this definition is not widely accepted, companies will need to pull the data for the calculation from their project budgeting and product revenue forecasting systems. Furthermore, it is unlikely that comparable data will be available from competitors and other companies.

Having offered these caveats about each measure, they all have some value for innovation scoring. New product sales as a percentage of current year revenue data may be available from your company's revenue systems. Industry and competitive data may be available from industry analysts or associations. Return on equity, profits per employee, and shareholder return data are widely available from analysts, the financial press, and company financial statements. Calculating return on innovation is likely to be a very time-intensive process for most companies.

» What percentage of your company's current year sales were generated by new products?
» What percentage of your company's current year sales were generated by new products compared to your company's average for the previous five years?
» Compared to your competitors, how does your company rank in percentage of current year sales generated by new products?
» What has been the trend in your company's return on equity over the last five years?
» How does this trend compare with your industry?
» What has been the trend in your company's profit per employee over the last five years?
» How does this trend compare with your industry?
» What was the percentage change in your company's split-adjusted stock price over the most recent five years relative to your industry?
» What was your company's return on innovation, as measured in NPV dollars, for its process and product innovations over the last five years?

If your answers to these questions fall far from the top, it may be particularly useful to analyze how well your company does on the four drivers of return on innovation.

LEADERSHIP

To answer the questions detailed below, a team could survey employees and managers to collect data on the effectiveness of leadership, the quality of the culture, the caliber of human resources, the extent of employee empowerment, and the motivational impact of financial and other incentives.

» To the extent that you ask employees and managers, how many express confidence in your company's leadership?
» What percentage of the CEO's time is spent with the chief technology officer?
» How many employees and managers feel a strong sense of pride regarding your company's market position?
» How many employees and managers feel that their colleagues are the best people in the industry?
» What percentage of employees and managers graduated in the top 10% of their college/university class?
» How many employees and managers enjoy working with individuals from different parts of the organization?
» How many employees and managers feel a strong motivation to outperform the competition in pursuit of company objectives?
» How many key employees and managers work long hours in order to meet corporate business objectives?
» Does your company provide incentives to employees and managers to learn about new technical areas outside of their field of specialization?
» How many employees and managers feel that they have the inclination, authority and responsibility to make strategic decisions in response to changes in technology, competitors and customers?
» How many employees and managers feel that the organization makes a significant effort to minimize the "internal bureaucracy" that distracts them from creating value for customers?
» How many employees and managers believe that the company provides them with tangible opportunities to achieve personal wealth and career objectives?
» How many employees and managers receive compensation that is linked to independently administered surveys of customer satisfaction?
» What percentage of employees and managers are covered by a stock option program?

If your company answers "none" or less than 25% to these questions, there may be an opportunity to improve your company's approach to leadership. In general, your answers may indicate that your company tends to follow a somewhat bureaucratic approach to managing people that makes it difficult to attract, retain, and motivate the best scientists and engineers.

TECHNOLOGY

To answer the questions detailed below, a cross-functional team could be created, potentially with outside assistance. This team could interview employees who are primarily responsible for technology management. The team could collect data on topics such as identification and valuation of core and non-core technologies; technology alliance formation, negotiation and management; and outsourcing/outplacing of non-core technologies. The collection of internal data could be supplemented with a review of industry analyst reports on the company and its technology.

» How many times in the last five years has your company formally identified and valued its core technologies?
» Does your company have a leading market position in any "leverage point" technologies?
» If yes, is the technology perceived by customers and industry analysts as the industry leader?
» Is there an individual or organization within your company that is solely responsible for monitoring new technologies?
» If yes, how many "paradigm shifting" technologies has this individual or organization identified and helped the company to exploit over the last five years?
» How many significant technology partnerships or acquisitions has your company executed in the last five years?
» How much of a reduction in product development cycle time would you attribute to these partnerships?
» What percentage of current year revenue would you attribute to these deals?
» How many technology outplacement transactions has your company completed in the last five years?
» Over that time period, how much capital as a percentage of your total R&D budget was attributable to these deals?

» How many technology outsourcing deals has your company executed in the last five years?

» Over that time period, how much capital as a percentage of your total R&D budget was attributable to these deals?

» What percentage of current year revenue would you attribute to these deals?

» How many of your company's non-core technology alliances over the last five years were initiated with clear, mutually agreed upon objectives?

» How many of your company's non-core technology alliances over the last five years were managed by executives with clear accountability for achieving these objectives?

» How many of your company's non-core technology alliances over the last five years exhibited strong cultural compatibility?

» How many of your company's non-core technology alliances over the last five years actually achieved the objectives set forth at the beginning of the alliance?

If your company answers less than 25% , below 2, or "none" to these questions, you may have an opportunity to improve your approach to technology management. In general, your answers may indicate that your company tends to follow the costly and time-consuming "Not Invented Here" approach to technology management.

PRODUCT DEVELOPMENT

In order to collect "valid" data to assess product development, a significant investment may be required. Specifically, the company could create a team to map the process for the development of a "typical" new product. This process map would trace the product development process. With the help of financial personnel, it could be useful to identify the time and cost by department associated with each process step. The team would also collect data covering a representative cross-section of projects to address issues such as project team composition and incentives, project planning, work with early-adopters, use of prototypes, and the effectiveness of the company's product supply capability. It could be helpful to supplement the review of internal operations with a survey of customer perceptions of these processes.

» How many of your company's new products over the last five years were developed by teams consisting of engineering, manufacturing, marketing, and other functional skills?

» In how many of these teams did the functional specialists work together from the initial research design to product launch?

» In how many of these research projects did teams work together to develop phased project plans with specific action steps, deadlines and managerial accountability?

» How many of your project teams received significant financial and career rewards for producing commercially successful projects on time and within budget?

» In how many of these projects did teams identify and meet with early-adopters to understand their specific unmet needs at the beginning of the design?

» In how many of the projects were prototypes developed based on the team's detailed understanding of the unmet needs of early-adopters?

» In how many of the projects did project teams redesign prototypes in response to early-adopter feedback, particularly after the first version?

» In how many of the projects did teams redesign prototypes in response to manufacturing and purchasing department feedback?

» In how many of the projects did teams redesign prototypes in response to marketing, sales and customer service department feedback?

» In how many of the projects did teams do market research to assess whether their product outperformed competitors in the attributes that customers valued most?

» In how many of the projects did this market research indicate that their product did outperform competitors in the attributes that customers valued most?

» In how many of the projects did the company experience a steady increase in product demand after the demand of early-adopters had been satisfied?

» In how many of the products that experienced such demand growth were manufacturing, distribution, and sales able to meet the demand without significant quality and customer satisfaction problems?

If your company answers "none" to most of these questions, you may have an opportunity to improve your approach to product development. In general, your answers may indicate that your company still follows a costly and time-consuming "relay race" approach to product development.

RESOURCE ALLOCATION

To collect objective data on your firm's resource allocation process, a similar team approach could be used. It would be particularly helpful here to compare projects that succeeded with those that failed. This comparison could pinpoint the highest leverage improvement opportunities.

» Do project teams conduct post-mortems after projects are completed to identify improvement opportunities?
» How frequently does your company use management offsite meetings and informal lunches to share learning across operating divisions and project teams?
» How frequently does your company use portfolio grids for analyzing corporate strategy?
» How frequently does your company use the same portfolio grid to screen research projects?
» How frequently do proposed research projects "survive" the screening process?
» Does your company use phased project plans that are organized to provide "exit ramps" before significant resource allocation decision points?
» Do project teams use activity-based costing to estimate the incremental net cash flows associated with each decision node?
» Do project teams estimate the probability of continuing and the probability of "exiting" at each decision point?
» Do project teams calculate project expected values by multiplying the probabilities and discounted net cash flows associated with each project?
» Does senior management calculate portfolio expected value by cumulating the expected values of each project?
» Do project teams perform sensitivity analyses of project expected value by varying the 20% of the input variables that drive 80% of expected value?

» Does senior management schedule portfolio review meetings to coincide with critical project decision points?

» Does senior management meet with project teams to offer advice on specific technical, regulatory, manufacturing, or marketing problems?

» How frequently does senior management agree with the resource allocation recommended by project managers?

» How frequently does senior management "kill" projects based on their failure to pass pre-determined trigger points?

» Do project teams update the probabilities and net cash flows of project decision trees as new information is uncovered?

If your company answers "rarely" or "never" to these questions, you may have an opportunity to improve your approach to resource allocation. In general, your answers may indicate that your company tends to make resource allocation decisions based more on internal politics than on measurable risk and return considerations.

CEO CHANGE AGENDA

The Innovation Scorecard can help companies analyze the extent to which they are following best practices in the business processes that drive return on innovation. If the Scorecard helps to pinpoint improvement opportunities, it is the responsibility of senior management to take advantage of these opportunities. Answering the questions presented here can suggest specific business processes for which the benefits of change are most likely to exceed the costs.

Meaningful organizational change is difficult, but often necessary if a firm is to survive over the long term. The process described below has been followed by many outstanding companies at critical points in their history, yielding outstanding results. The HP printer example, that created an $8bn a year business for the company, was detailed earlier. Ford Motor followed a similar change process as it developed the best selling Taurus in the 1900s.

If the results of a company's Innovation Scorecard indicate that its return on innovation lags the industry, its CEO could take the following steps.

» **Pick a "trial" division.** As HP did with its Vancouver Printer Division, a company could select an operating unit where competitive imperatives make change particularly critical. This division could become the site in which to experiment with and develop a new approach to product development.

» **Build a "change team."** The CEO could pick a team including this division's executive and key functional managers. The CEO could supplement the team with an outside resource to provide structure, tools and an objective analytical perspective on the team's work.

» **Develop a change plan.** To initiate the team building process, the CEO could give the team a deadline by which to produce a plan for changing the selected process, linked with the creation of an important new product for the company.

» **Map the current process.** One of the first steps in the plan would be to map the current process using a recent project as the example to study. The project mapping could be supplemented with detailed tracking of costs and time for each project step.

» **Study the process of "admired" companies.** The team could then identify and arrange to meet with companies that were selected for study due to their outstanding track record. Benchmarking could be arranged to enable the team to identify specific practices that could benefit the company. This data could be supplemented with the perspectives of experienced industry analysts.

» **Design a new process.** Based on an analysis of hand-offs and redundancies in the current process and the good ideas identified through benchmarking, the team could design a new process. The division team could then follow the redesigned process to achieve the project objectives.

» **Train the rest of the organization.** If the new process produces a favorable outcome, the "trial" division will need to make itself available to other divisions seeking to learn from its success. By providing a "living laboratory" within the company, the CEO creates the basis for evolutionary change that helps the company to enhance its return on innovation.

Frequently Asked Questions (FAQs)

Q1: Who are the technology leaders?

A: See Chapter 1.

Q2: Why are the technology leaders important?

A: See Chapter 1.

Q3: How do technology leaders sustain outstanding performance?

A: See Chapter 2.

Q4: How do technology leaders create success cycles?

A: See Chapter 2.

Q5: Where can I find cases that illustrate how technology leaders operate?

A: See Chapter 7.

Q6: How has the management of innovation changed over the last 100 years?

A: See Chapter 3.

Q7: How do technology leaders use the Internet in their business?

A: See Chapter 4.

Q8: What are the current issues in the management of innovation?

A: See Chapter 6.

Q9: How do I find out more about the subject?

A: See Chapter 9.

Q10: What can my organization do better as a result of the lessons from the technology leaders?

A: See Chapter 10.

Index